The SEN handbook
How to do SEN the right way

Greg Higman

First edition 2024

Copyright ©, Greg Higman, 2023
All rights reserved. No parts of this book may be reproduced without the written permission of the publisher. For more information and permissions, contact the publisher at higmangreg@gmail.com
All copyright holders of pictures included in this book have been contacted and permissions were granted to use this material.
Publisher's information: Greg Higman, www.senhelper.co.uk
All events and characters in this book are completely imaginary. Any resemblance to actual people is entirely coincidental.
ISBN: 9798874427184
Cover designed by santa cat design
Published by santa cat publishing, www.senhelper.co.uk

Dedications

This book is dedicated to all of the hardworking teaching assistants who have worked tirelessly and gone above and beyond their duty to support the children they work with.

For Temi Osinowo, who made a difference to many lives.

For Beth

For Jupiter

For Jane

Contents

Introduction and a word on structure

Section 1 - General advice
1.1 Get to know the kids first	11
1.2 Meeting the child's needs and documentation	15
1.3 Parental involvement	19
1.4 Triggers	28
1.5 De-escalation	31
1.6 The emotional check in	33
1.7 Boundaries	35
1.8 Physical contact	38
1.9 Consistency	42
1.10 Rules for day to day life	48
1.11 Modelling positive behaviour	52
1.12 Praise	55
1.13 Target setting	57
1.14 Contingency planning	61
1.15 Your own resilience and well-being	63

Section 2 - The Quick guide
2.1 ADHD (and ADD)	71
2.2 Autism	76
2.3 Depression	80
2.4 Self harm	89
2.5 Eating disorders	101
2.6 ODD	115
2.7 Dyslexia and the Dyslexia spectrum	125
2.8 Dyscalculia	128
2.9 Learning disabilities	131
2.10 Hearing impairment and visual impairment	135
2.11 Anxiety disorders	139
2.12 PDA	144
2.13 How SEN is classified	151
2.14 The standard classroom adaptation	156

Section 3 - The in depth guide

3.1 Safeguarding	160
3.2 Autism – another look	193
3.3 ADHD – another look	216
3.4 Dyslexia – further information	239
3.5 Attachment and attachment disorder	248
3.6 Behavioural difficulties and de-escalation techniques	262
3.7 Therapeutic practice	272
3.8 What do these job titles mean?	285
3.9 Unions and pay scales	297
3.10 Education health and care plan (EHCP)	301
Appendix one - Glossary	308
Appendix two - A relaxation technique	319
Appendix three - Further resources	324

Introduction (and why I have written this book for you)

The wonderfully interesting field of SEN is a fascinating environment to work in. No two days are the same and the SEN children can be very interesting souls to get to know. If you like a varied and interesting working day, SEN could be the right place for you.

Many children can have barriers to their learning, which can make progress challenging for them in one way or another. It is extremely rewarding when we help a child to do their personal best, or to overcome an obstacle in their path.

The schools that provide education for SEN children are extremely varied in the quality of what they provide to the learners; from places that are well organised, safe and well thought through to some schools which have a lot of catching up to do.

If you are working in SEN schools and with SEN children for a while, it is likely that you will see both ends of the spectrum of schools. This book will offer you realistic, down to earth advice and serve as your guide for how to *do things well* and will be a quick reference for advice when sometimes you have to adapt and think fast. You have chosen this book wisely.

I share my observation that some SEN provisions can be poorly organised for a distinct reason (not for the sake of simply grumbling) and I would like to point out to you the people who lose out the most in these environments - *the children*.

I sincerely encourage you to be part of the solution, rather than part of the problem.

Be a *child centred practitioner* and get into good habits in your work with the children, who can be disadvantaged and can have the odds stacked against them from day one in their lives.

SEN children are, in my experience, very influenced by their surroundings and the attitudes and behaviours of the adults working with them. A calm, supportive and nurturing environment tends to bring the best out in them, whilst conversely, a chaotic or poorly organised environment can often bring out the less positive aspects of them. This will become self-evident if you experience both types of practice in person. To some, this may appear to simply be common sense. There is lots of relevant information on how to have an easy and fun working day for both adults and children in the coming chapters.

Throughout this book I will give you as much useful, practical advice for how to do things the right way, and how to positively contribute to your workplace or home and ultimately towards better outcomes for the SEN children you interact with.

As we go along, I will point out a few red flags that generally indicate poor practice and I will also detail what good practice looks like in the modern workplace. Whether you are new to the sector or more experienced, you will benefit from keeping these in mind.

Being someone who likes a good reference book, I was quite surprised in the earlier part of my career, by the lack of a single decent handbook on the shelves of the book stores which I could put in my laptop case and use for general quick reference as I learnt day by day.

The books I found were often ponderous tomes of impractical academic research that whilst interesting, weren't of much practical use to me in the classroom or sometimes book length opinion pieces that equally missed the mark for my needs at that time. Neither really had the practical use for my daily work that I was looking for.

So, I present to you, the book that I would have liked to have had close to hand, to check and learn from, back when I was new to SEN (when sabre toothed tigers were far more of an everyday concern, naturally). Based on my personal experience of the right way and the wrong way to do things, but also informed by reliable, modern thinking and research in the field. I hope this book will help guide you through what can sometimes be confusing territory.

A word on structure

This book has an emphasis on education but the contents can also be useful for those who work in children's homes, are local authority workers with a foot in the SEN world and also parents with SEN children. So, this book can be used by a variety of different people, without a great need for extensive foreknowledge of the subject.

This book is not an academic text and so is not Harvard referenced or similar and does not have footnotes on every page. You are welcome to check out the research on the topics discussed here via search engine or even to carry out your own action research in your workplace. This book is intended to be accessible to all, be they completely new to SEN or someone who is experienced and is looking for fresh ideas.

Some of the advice about SEN contained here can also be applicable to adults. The challenges posed by some SENs to the individual may not significantly change over the course of someone's life. For example, a dyslexic child will become a dyslexic adult.

The first section of this book will address a few key themes around good practise; how to do things the right way for positive results and how not to fall into common traps. This is mostly practical advice and it should be used to inform what you do and how you should ideally go about it.

The second section of this book features a quick guide to some SENs that you are likely to come across and also some common mental health conditions. This section will be useful to you, because if you find yourself working with a child with a certain SEN or mental health condition and you are not experienced in that particular area, you can thumb to that section of the book and rapidly get some tips to use in your interactions with them, a brief overview of that SEN and advice about what are commonly used strategies for working with children with that SEN.

There is an emphasis on practical advice, i.e. things that YOU can do to support the child. If the child is supported and their needs are being met, you will often find that the day will run more smoothly and therefore, both adult and child will have an easier and more fun day with more positive interactions and less stress.

The third section of this book provides you with a more detailed look at some of the most common SENs and will provide you with a better understanding of what they are and some of the theories and questions around them. These will get you up to speed with some key concepts and current issues rapidly.

There are also chapters in the third section which look at some crucial subjects like *safeguarding* and other key concepts in education that will be very useful for you to understand and refer to. Safeguarding should be at the front of *everyone's* mind when working with children

You may also encounter some potentially unfamiliar vocabulary as we go along. Ultimately, it would probably be useful for you to commit as much of this to memory as is relevant to your role. It will help you to have a shared professional language with your colleagues for when you are discussing the children that you work with and the systems around them. Professionals from different fields who work with children will share some of this jargon and so it will help you to communicate with the broader team around the child.

If you don't feel inclined to memorise long lists of acronyms, rejoice! A glossary of terms is included in the back of the book for you to bookmark and refer to. This will make life a bit easier. Enjoy!

A shared language can help communication wonderfully. For example, if you are not from an IT background, you may have found it challenging to communicate effectively with the IT team, as the realm of computer science has such a specific language attached to it. SEN isn't quite that bad, but the field certainly has its own vocabulary and quite a few things to wrap your head around. There is no time like the present to get started with this.

Remember - sometimes taking a highly prescriptive approach of *"the child will do 'x', because I say so"* will be met by failure. Sometimes you must be flexible. Wisdom is knowing what to be flexible about and what to stand your ground over. Pick your battles wisely.

On this, it is useful to think of the non-negotiables in your classroom, things like using racist or homophobic language or bullying should be non-negotiables under any circumstances. other, lesser things like a child making an impolite exclamation when they stub their toe could be given a pass under certain circumstances. The children should be aware of what the non-negotiables are. Let them know where they stand and you will have a better chance of things going the right way.

Always remember that *some* SEN children may have suffered considerable trauma and abuse from significant adults in their lives (especially sometimes those in the SEMH category) and as a consequence, they may not trust adults or may not automatically give their trust to adults. It is **you** who will have to do the work to gain their trust, do not expect it as a given and do not be offended if the child initially does not warm to you; you will need to do the ground work there.

Section 1 - General advice

1.1 Get to know the kid(s) first

One of the most important things that I cannot overemphasise is simply getting to know the kids or teenagers that you are working with.

Do not overestimate the simple power of this exercise. In a class of 30 children in a busy mainstream school this can be challenging to do rapidly, but, if you are for example, assigned to work at the back of the class with a lone SEN child or a small group, the value of a friendly chat (if they will engage with you) will pay dividends in terms of your relationship with them and therefore how much you will get done with them and ultimately how easy a day you will all have.

Simply walking up to a child with, for example, ADHD or *Social, Emotional and Mental Health difficulties* (SEMH) who may be highly disengaged from education and possibly even unhappy to be at school and bluntly saying *"turn to page 60 - Algebra time"*, may not be met with the warmth and gratitude you may anticipate and expect.

I have witnessed a few good teachers and TAs, who have been very successful in mainstream settings, come unstuck with an excessively formal approach that has worked for them previously but is perhaps best suited to mainstream, grammar schools or 6th forms. If this is you, you may have to modify your approach a little to be successful in SEN. There is a time and a place for every approach; every tool for the task it is best suited for. The very formal approach can work well sometimes, but it is probably safest to start gently.

I recall a very nice teacher with excellent credentials lasting one day only at a particularly rough SEN school I worked at many years ago. I introduced myself to him at the start of his first day and offered that if he wanted any advice or support with the teenagers he would be working with to just give me a shout as I got on with them pretty well. He was politely dismissive of the suggestion, which was of course their prerogative to do so.

At some point during the third lesson of the day I heard a commotion going on, down the corridor from my classroom. I went to investigate and found the poor teacher looking exceptionally stressed as he had been physically ejected from his classroom by a group of angry teenagers who proceeded to barricade the door so that he could not re-enter the classroom.

Later on, when I asked the young learners what had happened, they stated that they did not appreciate the tone which the new teacher spoke to them in. They didn't phrase it *exactly* like that, but I think that encapsulates what they were communicating as feedback on that teacher's classroom technique.

The poor chap had blown it with the toughest kids in the school and rather than modify his approach and try to build bridges with them, he decided to move on to fresh pastures that very day, which was fair enough. I think he felt a bit intimidated by the unexpected strength of the response from this particularly tough crowd.

If you are working in a specifically SEN setting you will usually have far smaller class sizes which will allow you to spend more time getting to know the children and you will likely be spending a lot more time with the young people on an individual or group basis, which can occasionally be somewhat intense.

Find out about their interests and try to build some common ground with them. This is not completely essential but it has been known to fast track a student regarding you as being someone they want to interact with, to do more work with and to behave generally better.

Some SEN learners may have very specific interests. You *may* find this to be especially so with those on the Autistic Spectrum (ASD/ASC) but this is not automatically the case. Some common interests that have turned up a lot over the years in my career include, but are not restricted to.......... Pokémon, doctor who, horses or animals in general, computer gaming, contemporary music forms, dance etc.

Having a bit of knowledge about the things the children are interested in can be particularly useful. In all honesty and sincerity, I never for a second suspected that a very rudimentary knowledge of Pokémon was ever going to come in particularly useful in my career or in any area of my future, but we live and learn.

If you don't know anything about their interest(s) but try to fake it, they will spot that you are faking it quite quickly. You would often be better served by getting them to show you about it, if they are willing.

You could attempt an exploratory exercise like getting them to create a PowerPoint with you, or a poster, or even a comic strip on the area of specific interest to them. This can be a good way to open the channels of communication on the right foot.

If they are not very talkative you could get them to do an *'about me'* poster or PowerPoint to try and find some information out about them. You can ask your co-workers too, as not every child will be very forthcoming in a conversation with you.

If you have access to the planning and paperwork for a child, it is very useful to familiarise yourself with this thoroughly so that you can learn what observations have been made about the child and their differences and interests.

1.2 Meeting the child's needs and documentation on the child

You can hopefully find out the details about the child's needs and differences in a document called an EHCP (Education, health and care plan), if they have one. This is often put together by a specialist EHCP writer from a variety of documents and consultations about the child and then modified once per year so that it remains current and relevant. You can have an in depth look at this in one of the later chapters of this book in section 3.

Such a document is usually constructed from the input of various professionals, potentially including educational psychologists, healthcare professionals, occupational therapists, Speech and language therapists, social workers and there is usually a section detailing the child's views and their family's views.

This is a key document and ideally this should be somewhere that it can be accessed by staff. The EHCP may potentially contain confidential information, so have some respect for this and the right to privacy of the child or you could get in hot water. Certainly do not discuss a child's private information where other children can listen in or leave their documentation laying around where someone might potentially wander off with it. This can lead to some very serious issues.

Alternatively (and perhaps more usefully) the EHCP document can be condensed into a more user friendly summary or student profile for convenience of use. The SENCO or a similar qualified member of staff would usually prepare and circulate a student profile document giving you the most important details about the child. This could ideally include information such as:

- A pen picture of the child, i.e. a brief summary of their history (as appropriate to share).
- Their SEN(s).
- Their specific health needs - allergies, incontinence, personal care etc.
- Their educational attainment and levels.
- Subjects or activities they like and dislike.
- Ways to support them in the classroom.
- Specific interventions to meet their needs.
- Triggers.
- Strategies to calm the child if they have behavioural difficulties (de-escalation strategies).
- Various other things that are deemed relevant by the person preparing the document.

To be fair, having access to something like the document described above is not guaranteed. A well organised school will likely have something similar to this available to staff, but this may not be universally available.

If you find yourself in a situation where there is a lack of guidance available but you know the child has a specific SEN, turn to the *'quick guide'* section of this book and have a read about that particular SEN to get some general tips in record speed.

If you do have access to a document such as the one described above, always pay close attention to the advice on what you need to do to meet the child's needs and to keep them safe.

16

I encountered one school that refused to inform the support staff and the teachers of the SENs of individual children or to let them see the EHCPs, as they believed it might *'prejudice'* staff in how they interact with the child. I would personally regard this as a *large, glowing, levitating* red flag about that school and its management as it is essential to adapt YOUR approach to the different children rather than have a one size fits all approach and keep your fingers crossed.

> *"If a child can't learn the way we teach, maybe we should teach the way they learn"*
> Ignacio Estrada

If you work at an SEN school, there should always be some manner of group briefing on new children with SEN; this is certainly useful at mainstream schools too. This would often be led by the senco or a senior leader and would include some discussion of the child and their needs, as documented in the paperwork that should arrive ahead of them or occasionally with them. This should be done so that everyone is on the same page from the first time the child enters the school and knows what they are expected to do.

Some of this may consist of general advice about working with that child and there may additionally be some discussion around *interventions* that are to be delivered by specific members of staff. Interventions are a structured way of supporting a child with some particular area of difficulty and can be for a variety of things, such as:

- Specific deficits in learning or where a child has fallen behind in, for example, maths or English.

- To improve manual dexterity.
- To help with the development of speech.
- To help cope with anxiety.
- To help with anger management.
- Healthy social interaction and use of language.
- And a wide range of other things.

Usually if you are tasked with delivering an intervention, you should receive appropriate training, either from the SENCO, SLT or you should be sent on a course to upskill in this area so that you are feeling confident and well informed about how to deliver that specific intervention.

If you are asked to deliver a specific intervention and you do not receive any training or guidance on how to deliver this, it is not impolite to ask why this is the case. It is best to do so via email so you can capture the response, just in case you need to raise this point in the future or discuss the response with someone more within your organisation.

1.3 Parental involvement and parent(s) as partner in education

Not all children live with their parent, or parents. Not all children who live with their parent(s) are automatically better off for it.

Some parents can be very proactive in wanting to help their child and work in partnership with the school for positive outcomes, some are not at all enthusiastic to do so.

It can be worth reaching out to the parent(s), fosterer, care home staff etc to see what strategies they use with their children that are successful. You may get some really useful pointers that may not have occurred otherwise. This can also be a good way of developing consistency between home and school, where feasible. We will look at some methods you may find helpful to use with parents further into this chapter.

You may be surprised sometimes to discover that a child behaves quite differently in one setting to another and sometimes can present as a completely different child.

For example, at an SEN primary school that I worked at for a time, there was a child, early in years, in one of the classes who really had, credit where credit is due, model behaviour in school. Their interactions with their peers were measured, friendly and kind and they were well liked; they applied themself to all of their lessons, were pleasant to staff and was a good all-rounder at school. This kid really was a shining example of best behaviour.

I often used to scratch my head and wonder not only what were they doing at our school, with its emphasis on behavioural difficulties, but also if any of the reports of their extreme behaviours at home could possibly be about the same child. An evil twin perhaps?

Reports would come in of extreme behaviours around the seemingly model family home with respectable looking parents which seemed very inconsistent with the child that we interacted with at school. I really found this apparent *Jeckyll and Hyde* presentation quite puzzling. I maintained a healthy sense of curiosity about why the child could be presenting so differently in the two settings.

In retrospect I can clearly see why there was such a gulf of difference in the child's presentation in the two settings. The poor young kid felt at his safest at school. They felt cared for, they did not feel constantly at risk and their basic needs were met by the school team, consistently and in a timely fashion.

One day this child showed us some physical marks that his parent had given them whilst picking them up to throw against a wall as punishment. No wonder they would behave so differently at home. Social services had to be involved immediately and that was that.

Whilst the above example is extreme, it is useful to maintain a sense of curiosity if there are discrepancies around how a child behaves in different settings. There could be a reason. It is also useful not to be overly preoccupied with external appearances as the parent here was seemingly very respectable. On the other hand some parents can be absolutely amazing allies, even if sometimes they may seem *superficially* unlikely candidates.

At the same primary school, we had another child, of around 8, who had some reasonably strong behavioural difficulties that could cause disruption to the other children in his small class, on a fairly regular basis. He was a likeable kid with a healthy sense of humour and a strong sense of fun *when engaged*. There was possibly an issue that his teacher simply wasn't engaging his active little mind enough.

The disruption grew to a point where steps needed to be taken as his teacher was not coping well and was simply sending him to stand in the corridor for a chunk of every lesson. A staff meeting was called, which focused on how we could move forward with this child and what we could do differently to support them.

After some lengthy discussion, I suggested that we call in the parents for a meeting to discuss the child and how we might work together to meet their son's needs and get a positive outcome. A deathly silence fell across the meeting room, shared by teachers and TAs alike.

Having an inquiring mind I asked what the problem was. The team of adults who worked directly with the child flatly refused to attend any meeting with the parents of this child and stated that the father in particular had something of a reputation in the local area. The mother, similarly had a reputation but mention of the father elicited the most foreboding amongst the staff team at that school.

I dug a bit deeper and stated that if they were going to refuse to attend a meeting with the parents, they should have an extremely robust reason for doing so as this was part of their job.

I will state for the record that the teaching staff were, of course, completely misled in their assumptions about these parents and they probably shouldn't listen to spurious gossip about people. Putting gossip aside, I noted that there had been no allegations of poor parenting made at any point.

Early that evening, I rang the home number we had on record and introduced myself. I spoke to the father in a cordial, friendly and child focused way, exactly as I would any other parent of a child at one of my schools. I did not think once about the negative reports from some of the teaching staff.

I found the father to be highly motivated by his child's wellbeing, some common ground we certainly shared despite any other differences we might have. He agreed to come in for a meeting and stated that his partner would be in attendance also.

I invited the child's class teacher to come to the meeting and again they flatly refused, which I have to say I was fairly unimpressed with. I would do it solo then. The meeting arrived later that week. The parents came in and indeed, the father had the physique of a man who you might imagine pulling trees from the ground with his bare hands.

Their attitude was one of concern as they wanted their son to do well at school and they took a dim view of his recent behaviour. We discussed things like a daily handover from school to discuss the positives and negatives from their son's day and agreed on some shared strategies that we would both use and some shared targets around behaviour that we would work towards.

I thought I would push my luck and I asked if they would be interested in doing a course for parents on Autism, to help them understand their son's behaviour better. Rather than pulling one of my limbs off in one elegant movement, they were very receptive to this and did go on the course. We parted on good terms with handshakes and we did our bit as promised and so did they.

Between us, we managed to turn their son's behaviour around so that the child could express themselves in a more positive fashion and start to self-moderate and all before they hit puberty and quadrupled in size.

It's an important lesson, not to judge on appearances. There was some very negative talk about these parents, but we had some very solid common ground, that of wanting a good outcome for their kid.

This is not to diminish the fact that some parents can be very aggressive and even dangerous. I had the misfortune of having to square up to a physically large and very aggressive parent with some very serious issues, who had come onto the school grounds in order to assault a teacher who they felt had dealt unfairly with their son.

I had the unenviable task of having to stand my ground to this particular parent and telling them that the police had been called and if they did not vacate the school grounds within the next 20 seconds they would almost definitely be arrested and charged. They left sharply, as they did not feel strongly enough about the issue they had trespassed on the school grounds over, to be arrested and detained, which all said was quite fortunate.

In this instance their son had assaulted several other learners and a member of staff and so in keeping with school policy, they were held in order to prevent them from harming additional people. I supported my team's decision to physically hold the child as being proportionate (to prevent them from assaulting more people) even if their response was a little slower than would have been ideal.

Some children have been picked up by the system and are living in a children's residential home. The quality of children's homes can vary wildly as you will discover if you work with LAC (looked after children). You will ideally have regular contact with the staff at the children's home. The child may behave very differently in the two settings based on a variety of factors and causes.

One key thing to try and do with LAC kids, is, if the child is prone to some challenging or poor behaviour, get a handover from the children's home before they arrive on site. This may not always be possible, but it is a good thing to try and get a heads up if the child is coming in after a particularly unsettled patch.

For example……..

- A birth parent may not have turned up for contact because of substance misuse or other issues.
- They could have been in a fight with a member of staff in the home.
- They could have ongoing conflict or bullying issues with another child.
- Another child in the home could have had significantly dysregulated behaviour which has unsettled them.
- It could be a problematic anniversary for them, like the anniversary of being taken into care, an estranged parent's birthday or something else.

Being forewarned by the home that there is something up, before the child comes into school can pay dividends. You can modify your approach a bit. If this kid is having a really tough time, show some extra kindness to them; do an activity they like or simply be there to listen if they trust you enough to want to talk about things which may be difficult for them to process and deal with.

Think back to when you were a child, it is entirely possible if you are remembering clearly that there may have been times when you struggled to cope with something that was happening. Remember how that felt for you and show empathy for the child. Even if you had a picture book perfect childhood, think about what the child is going through and exercise empathy towards them.

You will occasionally get a parent or sometimes care home staff member who is not particularly qualified or experienced in education but will try and call the shots and tell you what you should be doing in school.

Always listen and take on board what they are saying, they may have some great suggestions, but make it politely clear that ultimately the school has to decide what should be happening in the classroom. Do not be tempted to do the wrong thing because a care home manager or parent puts you under pressure to do things a certain way.

There are various things which you can, with parental agreement, put in place to support and assist a child in developing and hitting their targets. For example....

- A report card can be sent home every day via email detailing how well they engaged in their classes and any positive or negative behaviours.
- A daily handover can be done via telephone or email (depending on what is most convenient) detailing how the evening before went for the child and how the day has gone, including any particular positives or negatives.
- A face to face handover in the morning and at the end of school if the parent (or carer) drops them off and picks them up from school.
- Regular meetings to set and review targets and progress.
- Rewards to be worked towards by the child for behaviour in home and school.
- A contract for the child between home and school.

So, when trying to work out how to best meet the needs of the child, do not neglect the parent(s)/ carer as an avenue to explore for support and advice. The best case scenario is that they could be valuable allies in helping the child to grow and blossom.

As a word of warning, some children are not allowed to have any contact with their parents or are only allowed to have very controlled contact that is supervised by social services.

In this case it is not impossible that the parent's contact details may still accidentally be on the school systems; there should at the very least be a note on there stating not to contact them, but you cannot be absolutely guaranteed of this.

Be aware of the risks and play it safe. If you think there is a possibility that a child may not be allowed contact with their parent(s), check with someone in management before contacting them.

1.4 Triggers

A trigger is something specific that can happen around the child that is likely to cause difficult feelings to arise, which may manifest in a variety of ways, including challenging behaviour.

Exactly why something is triggering to a child can be a complex issue. It can stem from early childhood experiences that possibly the child themself hardly remembers, it could be from a traumatic event that has happened more recently, someone doing something that they find annoying, or it could stem from a sensitivity to something that can happen in the environment around them. The possible causes are multiple.

Every child is different, but some things that could potentially trigger the children that you work with could be

- Getting in their personal space or making physical contact.
- Making demands of them that they find anxiety inducing.
- Mentioning family or family members.
- Specific anniversaries that they find difficult, eg, the date of a bereavement, the date that they were taken into care etc.
- Loud environments.
- Changes to established routine.

This list is far from exhaustive and you may be able to add another 100 possible triggers to it! But this should give you a few things to think about and a starting point to think about what triggers might affect the children you work with.

It is an extremely important aspect of your work to notice and take heed of the triggers that a child may have. Potentially you might work with a child with a volatile temper or challenging behaviour. Neither child, nor adult, nor peers (most likely), want them to go into a state of meltdown and become very upset.

If you are mindful of what triggers the child, then you may well be able to avoid *most* of the potential incidents during the day. So, a little effort in this direction can actually go a very long way!

When a child's trigger is pressed, you may see a range of behaviours from mild to extreme. Some possibilities are listed below:

- Tears.
- Depressive episodes.
- Violent outbursts.
- Running from the classroom or absconding from school.
- Self harm.
- Substance or alcohol abuse.
- Directed violence
- Vandalism.

Whilst not all SEN children will present with challenging behaviour, some can and it is important to understand what can cause or exacerbate this.

For example, if you know a child has a particularly challenging relationship with their father or mother, try not to mention parents around them. Let father's day and mother's day sail past without acknowledging them and certainly do not be the one to suggest that they make a glittery card for a parent who may have considerably traumatised them. I have seen this done in class by someone who really should have known better and the results were fairly explosive and resulted in a very distressed child. This could have been so easily avoided resulting in a nicer day for all involved. So be mindful of those triggers.

If the child wants to discuss challenging material from their past with you, be a good listener (and inform your line manager or DSL of what they share) but let them start these conversations unless you are a trained therapist and know what you are doing or you are following the instructions of a trained therapist who has written a coherent plan for you to follow. Many SEN children have happy home lives and do not have traumatic pasts, but do not assume that this is the case.

If you are aware of a child's triggers, you know to try and avoid those things, within reason, so as to not end up having an unnecessarily challenging day for both the child and you. If the triggers are unknown and you notice what some of them are, share this with other members of staff.

Of course, it is possible that a child may be triggered by recalling a difficult memory. You can't do much when that happens or necessarily see it coming, but still try to de-escalate them before things get too heightened if you can.

1.5 De-escalation

Another thing to try and be aware of is if there are known methods for de-escalation that should be used with that child. Very basically, de-escalation means methods for helping to bring a child back down to earth if they are getting angry, agitated, anxious or otherwise upset. There are various techniques that we will look at throughout this book, these are not guaranteed to work with every child but they are a good starting point to learn from and can certainly be worth a try.

The golden standard is to recognise when a child is beginning to become distressed and to de-escalate at that point, rather than waiting until there has been an incident and then trying to de-escalate them and pick up the pieces.

Some de-escalation methods will work better for you than others and you will need to be aware of what is considered 'within school policy' and what is not. For example, it may be appropriate to take a child out of class for 5 minutes at some schools so they can calm down by taking some deep breaths and having a change in activity, but it is not universally ok to do this, so be aware of what is considered standard practice at your setting and go with that for the sake of consistency with the other members of staff, unless what other staff members are doing is not good practice of course (in which case consider what you can do differently to them).

If you are lucky and your school is proactive, the child may already have a decent plan in place for de-escalation strategies that they can use. If this is the case, learn them, learn what they are and find out how these work in practice for the child. It may be the case with some children that they need to be directed and assisted in using their strategies by an adult. However, they may be mature enough to use their de-escalation strategies unprompted; some may not like to be reminded to use their strategies. Be aware of what works and what does not work for the child and sensibly modify your approach accordingly.

The ability to de-escalate a situation that is developing for a child is a very useful skill to have as it will make the school day run more smoothly. This is usually easier to do if you have a friendly professional relationship with the child already existing, as described earlier in the book.

1.6 The check in

If you work in a place where there is less opportunity for one on one time, you can still attempt an emotional check in. This is very simple to do. You could simply intercept the child (or give a member of support staff this job, if the child gets along with a particular member of support staff reasonably well) when they arrive in your class or at school and ask them how things are going. They may not want to talk, they may tell you something crucial which they have never disclosed to an adult before, or they may simply let you know that they are having a tough time. Hopefully at the very least this simple exercise may give the child the message that *someone* cares about them and is taking an active interest in their well being and life.

Be sure and let your colleagues know what you are doing and why, just so you don't give the impression that you are taking a special interest in that child over the other children at the school. Note down anything that they may say that is out of the ordinary and let your line manager or DSL know about it.

The emotional check in should be very easy to do in SEN settings where there are usually smaller class sizes. It can be written into a child's personalised plan that a trusted adult does the emotional check in every day.

The emotional check in can be classified as an intervention and it is regarded as such in some settings. The reason for its inclusion here is that it can be useful to use with a very wide variety of young people who have either SEN or mental health difficulties. The emotional check in can be used with most young people who are struggling a bit, be they depressed, Autistic or many other things. Please consider this method of support in general when you read through the advice for the conditions covered in section 2 of this book.

1.7 Boundaries

As well as making friends with the children we work with it is also extremely important to establish and maintain healthy BOUNDARIES.

Poorly maintained boundaries can lead to all kinds of issues for both you and the children you are working with and can even lead to your colleagues regarding you as suspect, even if the truth is you are just a bit inexperienced but actually a nice person. So, be aware of this.

Some people who are attracted to working in SEN or residential care may have had challenging experiences themselves as children, and sometimes that first hand wisdom and experience that there is light at the end of the tunnel, if a child is going through a difficult few years can be invaluable but it is extremely important never to let the lines be blurred and to compromise your professional practice.

Social media

Do not let the children you work with add you on social media or interact with you on social media under any circumstances.

It is better in all honesty if you use a fake name on social media because some of the kids will look you up. Don't have pictures online of yourself out partying on the weekend or anything like that as the children may find them and circulate them for a bit of fun, and this can seriously compromise your professional image at your school. Think smart with social media!!!

If you do make the grave error of letting children add you on social media you will raise suspicions in the minds of your colleagues when they inevitably find out and some of these suspicions can point towards you being of unsavoury character and may result in a formal investigation, formal warnings or even dismissal, so just don't do it.

One exception to the general rule about social media is where some social workers will have a work profile on social media that the children who they work with can contact them on. This account would be solely for their work and would be in line with their local authority's written policy. It is not smart for you to do this unless it is specifically your school's policy to do so, and it probably is not; or alternatively, your head teacher and DSL's written permission to do so.

Mobile Phones

Pretty much the entire population above a certain age has a mobile phone these days. Don't give the children you work with your personal mobile number unless someone's life depends on it and even then inform your line manager immediately that this has happened and the reason why it has happened.

Some schools provide staff with work mobiles or a work mobile for offsite activities. Make yourself familiar with your school's policies and procedures on this and follow them. Much like social media, if you are having text conversations with a child in the evenings, you are going to make yourself look very unprofessional and potentially a bit sinister.

Don't do it even if the child asks nicely. Also, don't take photographs of the learners, however innocently, on your own equipment. Use the school camera or a school phone if this is, for example, to document some work they are doing or an event they have put on or attended.

1.8 Physical contact

Your school may have a policy around this or it may be a section of another policy. Be aware of this and if you are not sure what you are supposed to be doing, ask a senior member of staff what the expectations are. Schools will differ quite a bit on this, but you are advised to err on the side of caution as problems can arise from even innocently intended physical contact.

If you are working in a setting with primary children, or children who present in their behaviour in a way which we might consider to be somewhat primary school (perhaps due to learning disabilities or similar), they may for example, attempt to sit on your lap.

Under no circumstances allow this. It will look very odd to your colleagues, if they are doing a decent job, and if you see your colleagues doing something like this, it should be reported to your Designated Safeguarding Lead (DSL) immediately. This could easily be viewed as 'grooming' or you could in fact be unwittingly preparing the way for unsavoury types who might do this as part of the grooming process.

If you are working with children with learning disabilities or attachment disorder, they may not have a well developed sense of boundaries in terms of personal space and physical contact. You will need to maintain good boundaries around this in order to set a decent example for them and also to keep yourself safe. It is ok to remind a child what is your personal space and what your boundaries are. Just be polite, but firm.

Physical contact may mean something very different to a child than it means to you. A child who has previously experienced abuse may see physical contact from you as a prelude to abusive behaviour from you and the outcome from that could be very unpredictable. Physical contact could also be misconstrued by a teenager that you are interested in them in an inappropriate way and this could equally have very unwanted repercussions. You are best off playing it safe.

Some children may seek to play fight with you. This is to be discouraged under all circumstances. A friendly 'We don't play like that here.' may be all that is needed. I have seen less experienced staff members go down the road of 'play fighting' or sparring with teenagers and it can actually very easily turn into a real fight if the teenager becomes emotionally dysregulated and you really don't want to be explaining that to your line manager, as it is not a good look. If a child wants to spar, they should probably go to a boxing club or martial arts club where they can do this in a relatively safe and structured environment in order to let off steam.

Additionally I have previously even known some residential care staff to play at 'wrestling' with the children in their residential homes in the evenings as an activity for a bit of 'harmless fun'. I was informed about this during the morning handover about one of the children by a care worker (a handover is a brief conversation between school and care staff where anything noteworthy from the night before or any important information is discussed).

I must confess that talk of *'child wrestling'* as an evening pass time really made me raise an eyebrow as to how appropriate and sensible that actually was, but I was not their line manager and as such could not directly tell them to stop doing this. I made a mental note to discuss it with their actual line manager in a meeting very soon (although it turned out that they were already aware of this and were ok with it).

Later that day, I made a point of speaking to the main child regarding the wrestling that had been happening in the home and they were very candid in their response that they felt very attracted to one of the female care workers and that they had been wrestling with her in order to make physical contact with her and that they had been doing so for their own personal sexual arousal.

I informed the residential care staff and their manager of what the child had disclosed immediately and they were fairly horrified to learn this. They had considered it, somewhat naively, to be an innocent activity and that no real harm could come from it. Needless to say that the only wrestling that occurred from then on was firmly on the television screen. I had a candid chat with the young lady about consent and finding someone a bit closer to her own age and being a smart girl, she didn't do this to residential staff again. Awkward, and so easily avoidable.

Play it safe with physical contact. Don't put out weird signals to the children you work with. If a child is upset or having a difficult time and you know that for this child, a hand on their shoulder is appropriate and they are ok with it, go ahead and throw in some comforting words too.

Know your own boundaries on this and if a child oversteps the mark with physical contact tell them firmly that they are invading your personal space. Be firm but friendly and consistent in your approach.

1.9 Consistency

This is a fairly key concept in education. It is vital that as much as humanly possible, the staff at a school are enforcing the same rules the same way and responding to the children in a similar fashion. Otherwise the kids can get some confusing messages, play members of staff off against each other and it can generally introduce problems into the mix.

If you find that some of your team do not behave consistently, it can be problematic to fix unless you are their line manager. You can have a chat with them, or bring the theme of consistency up in a staff meeting but it may not have the desired effect. It can of course be raised with management and hopefully they can offer some guidance.

At the very least, the space which you preside over can be consistent in its application of rules and approach; this way the children will at least unambiguously know where they stand with you and what is expected of them.

Sadly, I have known some members of staff in one school that I once worked at a very long time ago, to bribe children with sweets and even cigarettes (I kid you not) in order to get them to behave. This really is the epitome of the old cliché:

"Making a rod for your own back"

If this is part of the culture at a school you are working at, this is another serious red flag of incompetency. Always report issues to senior management and the DSL and hopefully they will take an interest, although unfortunately, this is not universally guaranteed and sometimes senior figures can even be complicit in such negative cultures.

Staff who bribe a child to behave in an agreeable way when the child, for example, shouts or kicks, embeds and entrenches those problematic aspects of their behaviour and the child is highly unlikely to make significant progress with moderating their own challenges and overcoming their barriers to learning. The problematic behaviours will become more deeply embedded and they will often exhibit negative behaviour simply because they want a cigarette or a chocolate bar.

This is an extremely short sighted method of behaviour management. Please don't do it. Other members of staff who do not adopt this approach may come in for, in more extreme cases, physical violence because they do not present a cigarette on demand. I have seen this flawed paradigm of behaviour management produce some relatively extreme behaviours in the children who had the misfortune to be in contact with those adults.

You may have difficulty approaching members of staff with issues like this about their practice and they may not be receptive to what you have to say, if so, ask someone more senior in the organisation to tackle this as they may have more luck than you. If the senior managers do not see an issue with this type of behaviour management, that's another big old red flag about that school.

It is good practice to have a reward system in place for the children, but this is something different to bribery and if done properly can be a good way of reinforcing positive messages and hopefully positive behaviours. In a decent and well thought through reward system, things are earned through prosocial behaviour and working hard in class.

Good consistency in staff responses and messages is far more productive than the poor practice I described previously. All staff should adopt a similar approach to managing behaviour and a consistent approach to the boundaries and rules in the school.

If there are daily briefings, these can potentially be useful times to discuss consistent approaches or to remind staff of the expectations. This isn't always going to go down particularly well with some people who are particularly entrenched in negative practice, but there it is.

Ideally, in the non-mainstream, smaller SEN school there should be an all staff briefing in the morning (maybe 10 minutes) and also one at the end of the day. This should follow an agenda ideally so that it stays on track.

The debrief at the end of the day can be a useful reflective space and a time for aligning strategies around the kids but it can also turn into a venting space where staff may take turns to complain about children for extensive periods of time; this isn't particularly productive in my experience and can even help foster a sense of negativity towards certain children amongst the team. Keep it focused with an agenda and general discussion.

If you work in a small team, for example, running one classroom or a single year group, make sure that at least you and your team are doing things consistently and sensibly even if the broader school staff may not be. You can hold regular briefings to coordinate, communicate and to keep your team's practice tight and synchronised.

Children can react negatively to changes in their learning environment, especially if there has been a lack of consistency in the staff team previously, because they may well simply enjoy messing around. I remember being a teenager fairly well and I was no different; it is my belief that some adults selectively edit their own memories of their teenage years and bemoan how the younger generation are so much worse than theirs was. There is some strong evidence from sociologist *John Muncie* to suggest that this is very much the case, if you care to read his very interesting work.

The bottom line is that children will get used to a more consistent approach from the team that works with them. They will know where they stand better, know what is expected of them more clearly, recognise the boundaries and hopefully learn to behave in a way that will set them up better for adult life. If a team is on the ball and is stepping in time together, desirable change can happen in a school remarkably rapidly.

I saw one group of teenagers nearly riot at the suggestion that school lunches would consist of healthy food from now on, rather than fried chicken and French fries followed by chocolate bars every day. Death threats were issued, plates were thrown and the situation, briefly, looked acute. Within a week the teenagers were happily tucking into pasta and salad and similar fare every day and within two weeks not a single teenager was mentioning their former diet of fried food and chocolate bars.

Question: *How was the seemingly unachievable achieved by mere unarmed humans?*

Answer: *Consistency in staff response and approach.*

I have seen occasions before where adults working with children have thought it a kindness to behave inconsistently for some reason, to not follow the rules or to maintain the proper boundaries. I cannot emphasise enough that this is *not a kindness* - you are not being a good professional by doing this as you are not helping set the young people up for adult life.

When they are out in the post 16 adult world, a different set of rules start to apply to them and if they do not understand that they have to modify their behaviour under certain circumstances they could get in an awful lot of trouble, including youth offenders or worse still, getting stabbed or something dire like that.

So really, it can be fairly high stakes. Do right by the children and help them out with consistency, genuine kindness, positive boundaries and reasonable rules.

I have seen young members of support staff (and the occasional teacher) sometimes 'go native' and begin to identify too closely with the children they work with, perhaps because they grew up in the same neighbourhood, were in the same gangs, or recognise themselves in those children. This is to be advised against. Whilst it is natural to like the children you work with and even healthy to empathise, there must be a clear line of professional conduct which you must follow, or there can be serious consequences.

I have seen some inexperienced members of staff covering for children or teenagers where there is quite clearly an issue, or even not reporting some quite serious incidents because they thought they had dealt with it sufficiently by themself.

This has even extended in my personal experience to an inexperienced member of staff covering for a child who had brought a knife into school to threaten another child with.

This is an extreme example and it was highly irresponsible. This action dangerously crossed the lines of professional conduct and professional boundaries. There was no consistency with the anti-violence and anti knife crime message that was core to the school's values. This could also have had life changing consequences for some poor unfortunate.

If a child is starting to carry knives or something serious like that, there must be an appropriate intervention made. You could seek advice from the professionals network around that child if there is one or make a referral to a specialist who can deal with it or even just involve the police. Your school should ideally have a policy on this, read it and follow it. If there isn't a policy or some kind of guidance for you, ask someone senior why not.

Play it sensibly at all times and report *anything* dodgy that happens in your school. No exceptions.

1.10 Rules for day to day life

Whether you work at a mainstream school, a children's home, an SEN school or even a youth club, there are going to be certain behaviours that you don't want to see between your walls (and hopefully not outside of them either but you can't necessarily exert much influence over what a child does in the evenings).

Sometimes children have not had very positive role models which can potentially result in them having difficulties moderating their own behaviour. Sometimes children may have positive role models, but due to the nature of their SEN, traumatic experiences or other external influences, they are struggling to maintain a decent standard of behaviour. There can be various possible reasons.

Either way about, having a very clear and simple set of rules agreed, upheld consistently by staff and on display in a prominent place can be quite easy to do. This may be one of the first things that a child in a heightened state seeks to tear down from the wall to make a point so it can help to have them laminated, painted on the wall or behind Perspex.

This should include some non-negotiables, for example.....

- Treating the people around you with respect.
- Not vandalising the school environment.
- Not smoking or vaping on the school grounds.
- No bullying.
- Respecting diversity and difference (no hate speech).
- No mobile phones in class.

A session can be set up where the young people can discuss the school rules and can have lively discussion and debate about them, sometimes this works well in a PSHE class, form time or circle time - whatever works for your local setting.

I hosted a discussion around these themes in the format of a talk show a couple of times, which could have gone quite badly, but the teenagers really went for it, talking to the invisible microphone and offering some very insightful opinions and takes on what we were discussing. It could have fallen quite flat of course, but I already had a friendly rapport with those young people because I had put in the groundwork previously, which made them more likely to engage in the activity.

It should probably be pointed out that the list above is not completely exhaustive and a policy around the school rules should be available to staff and students on the school website. What you have on the wall in the classroom should be very condensed and easy to digest.

There should certainly be a *"code of conduct"* that applies to staff as well as rules for the children. This could be available for the children to see if it is appropriate to do so. This way, they can see that rules around acceptable and unacceptable behaviour apply to everyone, not just them. If the code of conduct is reasonable and you are following it, this theoretically shouldn't be too much of an issue. For example, are you vaping on school grounds on the sly? You really shouldn't be. Serious question, is that really the best example to be setting?

The students can be encouraged to write up their own model set of school rules. Some will engage in this seriously and some may struggle with the activity. In either case it starts a discussion about limits on behaviour.

Staff can agree to pick a focus area from the school rules to work on if there is some difficulty amongst the students in that area and then work consistently to a plan which is devised in staff meetings to reinforce that message or to promote the students adhering to that area of the school rules.

It is extremely important to establish boundaries around acceptable and unacceptable behaviour in the classroom, workshop, home or anywhere else you are.

These boundaries should be put in child friendly language that the children can understand. The rules should be interpreted and upheld in the same way by all of the members of staff so that the children know where they stand and there aren't any mixed messages being given out that can undermine your good work.

The phrase *'because I say so'* is unlikely to be consistently effective when working with children, especially those who can become dysregulated and oppositional. *'Because it is the school rules'* is a bit more effective. A better approach, in my opinion, is to explain to the child *'I can see you are feeling a bit unhappy at the moment but that's not the way we like to do things here, because.......'.*

Sometimes children may be going through a rough patch in their life and may significantly struggle with boundaries and behaviour because of this; in a mainstream school setting you may be completely unaware of the utter turmoil that may be going on for a child every time they walk out of the school gates, but as the adult in the situation it is part of your role to remind them and try to guide them in a supportive and caring way of what the boundaries are, and importantly - always listen to what they have to say. You don't have to agree with what they have to say, but you wouldn't want to miss something important that they are potentially telling you.

1.11 Modelling positive behaviour

It may seem an obvious thing to point out, but all of the adults working around and with children should model the type of behaviours that they want the children to develop. This is especially true if the children are behaviourally challenged or have developmental difficulties which can cause them to struggle with some prosocial/ positive behaviours.

Set a positive example by the way you act in front of the kids. If there is a no mobiles rule for the children, don't get your phone out and click around on social media. It undermines what people are trying to achieve. Model things like good manners to the children and your co-workers.

Some of the children that you work with in your career may not have had what you might consider positive role models in their early years whilst they were learning how to interact with the people around them.

Children learn a lot of the social skills that they use from their primary caregivers at a very early age - let's face it - they copy what we do.

If the children have not seen things like negotiation taking place when people have different ideas that may be in conflict (i.e. 'I want to play tennis' versus 'no I want to play a board game') then they may not understand this skill and may simply resort to more blunt tactics to get their own way. If there is a deficit in something like this, positively model this behaviour in front of the children (you can contrive it for their benefit even); do an assembly or starter on it and then encourage them to use this skill and sensibly reward it.

Here are some things that there could be a deficit of in children that you work with that you could model for them to hopefully emulate
- Taking turns
- Sharing a toy.
- Negotiating an activity to take place.
- Dealing with disappointment.
- Resolving a disagreement without conflict.

On the subject of 'good sportsmanship' I do not personally believe that overly competitive activities are good for children in general. Overly competitive activities can cause conflict, fall outs, even bullying. I favour collaborative activities where the children can share skills, work together, do problem solving as a group, negotiate and so forth. These are actually invaluable skills that they can use throughout their adult life. Shouting at each other and denigrating each other over 'missing a goal' or similar is in my humble opinion, not the most constructive way for the children to be steered or to express themselves.

If you do competitive sports with the children, talk about the value of positive behaviour (or 'good sportsmanship' if they prefer that phrase) in the activity and reward that positive behaviour with bonus points or verbal reinforcement rather than simply praising whichever kid is the most athletic (possibly by virtue of the speed of their development) or to put it another way possibly making a child who is asthmatic or similar feel bad about themself.
Competitive sports can be an opportunity to embed negative behaviours that may already be present, or they

can be an opportunity to help positive behaviours grow and take root in the psyche of the child. It depends broadly on how you handle these things.

Consider how you structure these activities and do not be afraid to set individual targets for the children that reflect their needs when you get to know them. You can remind the child what their target is in a supportive way and help them work towards achieving the target in their behaviour.

The children that we work with can be a bit more malleable and less set in their ways than adults sometimes, so you can actually be the positive catalyst that makes a real impact on the child's behaviours and therefore can have a positive impact on who they will develop into as an adult and ultimately how they will interact with the world around them.

You can help shape them into being positive and productive people who have prosocial skills rather than antisocial behaviours and potentially have a happier outlook in life and give out a more positive charge in the world because they can learn how to resolve things without conflict.

There can be many, many different things that you can do to model positive behaviour around the kids. Simply being friendly, kind and approachable are all good behaviours to model.

1.12 Praise

Some children will not accept praise. It is relatively rare but it is worth being aware of. Some children may have lived through traumatic experiences or have specific SENs such as ODD (covered in the quick guide section later in the book) which may cause them to not accept praise, sometimes aggressively so. If you are made aware that a child you are working with comes under this category, keep it in mind, be considerate and act accordingly. Find out how you can tailor your approach to meet the needs of that particular child.

To *most* children praise is a great thing. There *may* have been a lack of it in their life and so the child might not believe that they are actually good at much. This is sad but true. Some children's self-image can be quite low and even distorted which can lead to serious problems developing as they age.

Praise should be given freely to children who can accept it. Achievement is a very relative thing in the arena of SEN education. An able and calm child may excel at many aspects of school life and may set the bar quite high for their personal achievement. Another child may struggle to remain in their seat for more than five minutes at a time or another may struggle to paste cut out pictures onto a sheet of paper. Achievement is relative to the learner and their abilities.

Give praise freely for achievement. Most of us feel good when we are told we have done something particularly well and that praise may echo within our minds for some time, improving our well-being and happiness.

Verbal praise should be given to the children that you work with on a regular basis but not only for the school work that they do. When they exhibit prosocial behaviours, especially the ones which you may have set targets for, you should offer positive verbal reinforcement in a way that is meaningful to the child.

For example:
- *'That was definitely the right thing to do'.*
- *'I can see you tried your very best with that and you should be proud of yourself'.*
- *'You showed a good level of maturity there'.*
- *'I think you made the right choice there'.*
- *'You are setting a really positive example for the younger kids'.*

There are many possibilities, get to know the kids and use praise to reinforce positive behaviours and good application to their work.

1.13 Target setting

"A journey of a thousand miles begins with one step"
Lao Tze

I don't know about you, but I have always thrived on a well-defined target. For example, if someone was to give me the instructions, *'make things better'*, I could take any number of meanings from that statement as it is fairly nebulous. If it came to a point where we could sit down and review my progress towards that target, to see if I had *'made things better'* or not, I could boldly proclaim that I had and point to various examples but they may not agree with me.

However, if the language used had been more precise, and more intelligently phrased, for example by saying something like, *'improve your local environment by planting 20 trees'*, or *'when you feel overwhelmed, use your designated chill out spot and relaxation strategies'*, it suddenly becomes quite simple for me to understand what is expected of me and what the target being set is.

Target setting can be a valuable tool for us to use with the children we work with. If the child clearly knows what is expected of them and what they are working towards, they have a far better chance of actually achieving it.

If we set targets for the children we work with that are meaningful to them and useful for their development, we are onto a winner. Often when setting targets we use the acronym SMART. It isn't something to get completely hung up on, but it is very useful to consider SMART when setting

targets for the children we work with. SMART stands for (and I have seen a few different versions of this that mean pretty much the same thing)
- Specific
- Measureable
- Achievable
- Realistic
- Time constrained

We can consider the above when writing targets for the children we work with. Are the targets we are setting smart? Of course we all want Billy to achieve great things, but great things are generally achieved one step at a time, each step *a target*, if you will.

A good lifecycle for target setting for SEN children in school could be the term/ half term structure, if your school follows that pattern. For example, a target, or group of targets, could be set at the start of term. The target setting should ideally involve the child if they are able to participate in this. If the parents/ carers are friendly and amenable, then there is no reason not to involve them as well. There could be a friendly discussion with the child where the targets for them are 'negotiated' and their input is welcomed. They could even be invited to set a target for themself if they are able to participate in this.

Once the targets are agreed, they are committed to some manner of record. This could be a spreadsheet to monitor the child's progress, a database or a paper based system if you prefer. All staff can be made aware of what the child's targets are and can gently support them to meet this. Thus the child is more likely to achieve their target.

The targets would then be reviewed after a set amount of time, for example 6 weeks or 3 months. You would then use some kind of grading system to see how secure the child is in that target. For example, you could use:
- Green - has achieved the target completely.
- Amber - has achieved the target partially.
- Red - has made no progress towards the target.

Or, if you are more numerically inclined and like a tidy spreadsheet, you could go with something like (and maybe use a formula to total up their progress over the course a year)
- 2 - has achieved the target completely.
- 1 - has achieved the target partially.
- 0 - has made no progress towards the target.

The child can ideally be involved in the review stage of their target. This should **always** be constructive though. If the child has done poorly in working towards their target, do not focus on the problems, rather, focus on the solution. Sit and discuss what went well and encourage them to reflect on what could have been done differently.

As someone who has been hired to fix issues within schools many times before in my career, it can be overwhelming to look at a school with a hundred issues that need fixing. The only way to approach this is to break a larger problem down into individual issues. You then prioritise which of these is the most urgent and then target that particular problem. There may not be a quick fix but with consistent effort, you will finally get a lot of things sorted.

Working with children is not so different. If we have a kid who has a lot of behavioural difficulties and challenges, we probably aren't going to solve everything by clicking our heels together three times and saying a magic word. The likelihood is that we will make small but significant progress, regularly, through sensible target setting and all staff pulling in the same direction to support the child, with the child being fully aware of what is expected of them. The strategies for support should be well understood and known by all staff and the strategies the child must use should also be well understood by them.

1.14 Contingency planning

When I provide training and support for teaching staff, I always encourage them to do a little contingency planning. Back when I still did regular classroom teaching, I prided myself on maintaining something that I called the *'rainy day folder'*. In actual fact this was a USB stick, but let's not split hairs!

Sometimes the best laid plans can go awry - this is life! Sometimes a teacher may be taken ill or unexpectedly called away and you may have to step in and cover their classes, perhaps at zero notice. You may even not have any work set out for you and may be tasked with improvising.

The most successful people in life, in my opinion, are those people who plan ahead. You should plan ahead for occasions when you may have to step in and improvise - prepare some fun educational resources and keep them stashed somewhere that you can easily access them, be it a paper based folder, a USB stick or other electronic storage space or device.

I once found myself in the unenviable position of having to cover a primary class I had no foreknowledge of or work provided for, for two long days. Luckily, I had planned ahead for such unforeseen contingencies, and I had my rainy day USB stick in my bag. On this I had some interesting PowerPoint presentations about the solar system, which I was able to adapt to the age group and to get the children in the class very fired up about, through a dramatic delivery.

What followed was two days of cross curricular activities based around the solar system - Science, English (creative writing), art and various other activities that were both educational and also fun enough to get all of the learners on board and enthusiastic about.

It is a minor, but good piece of advice:

Always have a plan B close to hand.

It may alternatively be that a planned activity cannot happen for one reason or another. An activity may have been rained off or a school trip may have been cancelled due to a couple of students going into an advanced state of meltdown. Always have plan B to hand so that the day can proceed without any panic. It is always best if you can get on with things in a calm and collected fashion without breaking so much as a sweat.

1.15 Your own resilience and well being

It is important to be aware of your own emotional state and personal well-being whilst working in an SEN setting (or anywhere else for that matter).

Know yourself

It will differ wildly from one setting to the next what type of children you are working with but it is entirely likely that at some point in your career, you may find yourself working with children who have sad back stories or who may be going through extremely difficult times in their young lives. This may be more frequent with children who are 'Looked After Children' (LAC), children classified as SEMH (Social, Emotional and Mental Health) or children who have suffered significant trauma in their past. Or you may find that something upsetting happens out of the blue. It is difficult to predict.

If you do find yourself working with these types of children it is entirely possible that you may hear stories which you could find quite distressing (or which may trigger painful memories in yourself) or you may see behaviours that you may find difficult to cope with, such as self-harm for example. You can't unsee something, you just have to learn how to process it and deal with it in a sensible way.

If you have had a difficult experience in your working environment or a series of them, it can sometimes be difficult to 'shut down' after work. You may walk out of the building and get on the bus (perhaps even with this book by coincidence), but you can't always leave your feelings neatly at the school door to pick up again the following day.

After all, we genuinely care about the well-being of these children and when we see things not going so well for one of them despite our best efforts it can be distressing. We are only human after all.

Earlier in my career, I personally found that the concern and sadness I felt sometimes about an individual child's past, present or a bad outcome for them would follow me home and I might end up feeling despondent during my time out of work and sometimes I would find it challenging to compartmentalise a difficult day and to just enjoy my evening doing the things that I like, for example playing instruments, watching films or playing with my cats.

Carrying the negatives home with you can be a very dangerous habit to get into. You should not spend your evenings or weekends obsessing or stressing out about something that happened during your working day. It is something I did early in my career, but it is a habit I got out of. If you are doing this, you need to start to train yourself to not do this. Too much attachment can lead you to sadness. Remember that.......

You are not personally responsible for everything in the world.

Do not set out to boil the ocean - you will always fail.

The way I got through times like that earlier in my career was to do the absolute best job I possibly could and leave no effort unspent in trying to help the children out. That way, if things didn't turn out as well for a child as I might have hoped, at least I could sleep with a clean conscience knowing that I had done everything I could to try and help a positive outcome happen. This is a habit I have kept to throughout my entire career.

However, regardless of how much passion and effort you put into your work, sometimes the dice just don't roll the way that anyone wants them to, and you can be left with some difficult feelings. This is only human but it is essential to find a constructive way to deal with difficult emotions.

After all, this is what we want the kids to learn to do, right?

I will give you an anonymised example from my past. Many years ago, I worked with a teenager who had suffered some particularly serious, harrowing and protracted trauma. Theirs was a genuinely sad story and I resolved to do everything that I could to help this kid get through the very tough patch that they were in.

They suffered with suicidal ideation, depression, regular and serious suicide attempts, overdoses, cutting themselves quite deeply (even on their own face sometimes), attempts to drink cleaning products if there was a window of opportunity (this never happened on my watch as they were always safely locked in the COSHH cupboard as was policy), mood swings, bulimia and a host of other very challenging problems. Poor kid.

They had previously attempted to do some very serious harm to other adults who had worked with them in a different school to mine. This gave me pause as to whether they should be accepted to my school or not, but weighing it up, the risk levels seemed tolerable to me. I would never put my team at a level of risk that I would not be comfortable being in myself as a matter of personal policy.

We never actually saw any of those violent behaviours towards staff in our school, not on one single occasion. I sincerely believe that the reason we never saw these behaviours is because we had a genuinely therapeutic, child centred approach and all of the team were following the type of advice which I gave as a manager and also give for you in this book.

It was obvious that the kid actually liked being in school and enjoyed interacting with the team. I think it was probably the happiest part of their day at that time, and they were going through a very tough few years.

For all of the terrible stuff that had happened to this kid, they remained capable of being remarkably upbeat and philosophical about their existence a lot of the time, they had a strong sense of fun, had a sharp sense of humour and picked things up rapidly in class and liked to help others.

Their behaviour would fall a bit short of the school's expectations sometimes but they would be open to discussion and they had an uncanny knack of trying to do things differently the next time. We don't ever do favourites, but they were well liked by the other students and all of the staff. It was difficult not to like them.

The problem was, for whatever progress they would make in the school environment, their behaviours would become increasingly extreme in the residential home they lived in and anywhere else they were; places that my team and I had no influence on.

Eventually one of their later suicide attempts nearly succeeded and I found myself sitting with them in hospital making small talk and trying to lift their spirits a bit with lame jokes. After a series of psychiatric assessments they were deemed to be at too high a risk to themselves which led to them being sectioned.

The last time I walked away from the mental health hospital they were residing in, I felt a deep sadness envelop me, one that I would struggle to shake for a while. It was a bad time for that poor child but it was also not a happy time for the team who were similarly depressed and upset by what had happened.

When I examined the support that the school had put in place, I can honestly state that there was nothing more that we could have done to help this child. Nor had any member of my team let them down; they had done absolutely everything they could to help them, and I told my team that too. I told them in the staff briefing that they had gone to superhuman lengths to help this kid and they should be proud of that, but sometimes there isn't anything that we can do. Of course, we should *all* always reflect and think if there is anything that we could do differently to be better professionals, but this shouldn't involve beating ourselves up over things we can't change.

I think if we had given it less than 100% we would have had cause to do quite a lot of self-blaming and would have felt a whole lot worse.

Inevitably at some point in your career you are going to come across something that causes you upset. This is life. It may happen once or it may happen many times depending on the sort of place(s) you work and the roll of the dice.

Know yourself and be kind to yourself
(and also always do your very best)

If you are starting to take an emotional bashing, talk to someone about it. Talk to a trusted co-worker. Talk to a counsellor (your employer may pay for this). Ask older and more experienced members of staff if you feel that they might have good advice to give. There may be someone in your workplace who can signpost you to appropriate support if you're struggling. There may be someone outside of work who you can turn to for advice - talk to them, and don't keep the problem to yourself.

If you hit a point in your career where something happens which gets you off balance, don't bottle it up and certainly don't try to self-medicate with booze or anything like that. Meditation, Raja Yoga, Jogging, mindfulness, dancing, whatever sensible that works for you, do something different that might help you to be able to deal with difficult feelings.

In one of the appendices at the back of the book I give you a relaxation exercise that is extremely useful if practised on a regular basis. It definitely works. Skip to that section now if you want. You can do this exercise with the children you work with too after you have learned how to do it properly. Care for the children you work with but you must also care for yourself or you will burn out in one way or another.

Ultimately, give yourself some slack, and be kind to yourself. If you genuinely did everything you could, if you were kind and professional, you have nothing to beat yourself up over.

Section 2 - The Quick Guide

This section can be read in a linear fashion but is designed so that you can just turn to the section on a subject or SEN that you need some quick information on and read, in order to get some condensed advice on working with a child with a particular type of SEN. There is some more in depth information on some common SENs in section 3 of the book which you can study when you have sufficient time to go a little deeper.

Always go with the planning around the child if you have it! Sometimes the planning isn't very good, sometimes we aren't given it, and sometimes we are just thrown in at the deep end for one reason or another and have to improvise. Keep this book to hand and good luck!!

The conditions covered in this section are a mixture of SEN and some of the most common mental health conditions that you will come across in schools. Both are included here as a decent knowledge of things like self-harm, eating disorders and depression will help your interactions with the kids and the quality of what you provide for them.

You may encounter these conditions on a fairly regular basis both in mainstream education and in SEN education, so it is fairly important that you have a grasp of what these are and what you can do to support children who may be experiencing these difficulties.

Please remember that some of the subjects covered here, can potentially be triggering, perhaps more so if you have direct experience of some of the issues raised.

2.1 ADHD (and ADD)

ADHD (Attention Deficit Hyperactivity Disorder) is a neurodevelopmental condition; if you are born with it, you will usually have it for life. ADD is no longer really used as a diagnosis but you may still see it used sometimes. Approximately one in thirty people are thought to have ADHD.

The upshot of this is that if you are working in a mainstream school, statistically speaking, there is likely to be an ADHD learner in each class. Of course the statistical distribution of such things is rarely quite so even, but you get the idea. ADHD is fairly common and so having a good understanding of it, what to expect and some strategies you can try is going to be useful for you!

Most will agree that ADHD learners tend to have some of the following, although it is important to remember that different children (and adults) will have an emphasis on one or more of these traits rather than having a flat or equal amount of each. Everyone is different.
- Overactive behaviour (hyperactivity).
- Impulsive behaviour (impulsivity).
- Difficulty in paying attention and distractibility (inattention).

General advice

The following are some general pointers for how to effectively work with a child or teen with ADHD. These are not absolute rules chiselled into the very fabric of reality, but good guidelines that are the best advice I can give to

71

someone who is not already well versed in working with ADHD children.
- Get to know the child.
- Be clear on rules and boundaries and be consistent.
- Follow a routine. ADHD children can feel safest in a predictable space where they know what to expect.
- Help the child to organise themselves and encourage them to practise these skills.
- In your communication, be simple, clear and direct.
- Break tasks down into smaller steps - this can be written on a whiteboard, display or on paper for the child to refer to.
- Reward prosocial and positive behaviour (this can be verbal or according to a points system if your school has one).
- Allow slightly longer for tasks to be completed.
- Consider where the child is seated. Are they in a place with the least distractions to them? For example, noisy students, windows, doors to the corridor? They should be sat near to you so that you can monitor if they are starting to lose focus on what they are doing.
- Give them a limited number of positive choices; eg, *'we can now play a board game or watch a music video'.* Do not give them free reign to do anything as they may well find this overwhelming and it will likely cause problems.
- Give the ADHD child *special responsibilities* in the classroom if they can cope with it. This could be handing out books to the other learners; it could be taking notes down on the white board or drawing a diagram on the board for the class. This is essentially a movement break and it may help them

channel restless feelings more effectively and may improve self esteem.
- If the child does not already have strategies to cope with feelings of being overwhelmed, take the time to help them develop these.
- If the child lives with their parent(s) and their parent(s) are approachable, it can be a good idea to build a relationship with home to find out what strategies work there that could be used in school.

For learners with ADHD, we should always use the standard classroom adaptation as given towards the end of section 2.

Break the task down

When setting a task for a person with ADHD to do, it can be useful to break it down into steps for them. This can take the form of a bullet point list that you might write down for them to refer to, or they may be coached to write down for themself.

If you are teaching the class, it can be very useful to type out a few notes in a PowerPoint presentation as you go along or to write a few bullet points on the white board. This way your learners can refer back to this as they work to complete the task.

Expecting someone with ADHD to remember a sequence of steps to accomplish a particular task and then to execute them, can be over ambitious and it may serve to put them under less pressure by simply leaving some instructions on the board for them to refer to.

By making a simple adaptation like this, you may actually help the ADHD learner to stay on task, stay more focused and to possibly make a more positive contribution to the classroom environment.

Try not to overwhelm your ADHD learner. If an ADHD learner becomes overwhelmed, this can be expressed by them in what you may perceive as negative or disruptive behaviours.
Instead, break large tasks down into smaller bite sized chunks that they can more readily cope with. This way the ADHD learner may achieve proficiency at learning a new skill or in accomplishing a set task.

Movement and movement breaks

ADHD learners can have a great deal of difficulty in simply sitting still and their desire for movement can become very strong. Have realistic expectations for your ADHD learner(s). Attempt to figure in movement breaks for them. This can take the form of
- The child being allowed to leave their desk for a short period of time in some agreed way.
- The ADHD learner can be given the task of helping with practical demonstrations.
- Being given small errands to run, such as collecting books, collecting finished work, being in charge of a timer for a time constrained task, giving out books or pencils or other items that are to be used in the class.
- Having a designated movement break that is agreed with the teacher that can happen at a

designated time or can be agreed with the teacher at a suitable time.

> One class that I taught had quite a few ADHD learners in it. We developed a strategy between us of occasionally doing jumping stars in class when they were getting a bit restless (the non ADHD learners actually enjoyed this a lot too). Whilst this may sound bizarre, it actually worked very well for this group of learners.

In between learning tasks or if they appeared to be struggling to focus, I would ask if they wanted to do a set number of jumping stars, which they found to be fun and generally amusing as it was not something they had been encouraged to do in class before - they had simply been told to sit still and work. Naturally this was done in a safe manner away from things which the learners could harm themselves on and was included in the risk assessment for my classroom.

The gain from this is that the ADHD learners were allowed to do what their impulses were telling them to do in a controlled and safe way without causing disruption or difficulty. This may not work for all learners but can be something to try.

Thinking outside of the box for your learners can sometimes pay off. There are several more adaptations and techniques that you can try with your learners in the longer section on ADHD in section 3 of this book.

2.2 Autistic Spectrum Condition

Also known as Higher or lower functioning Autism, *'Asperger's syndrome'* (ASC/ASD) Autistic Spectrum Condition/Disorder etc.

This is a developmental condition, meaning that if you are born with it, you will continue to have it throughout your life. It is rooted in a minor difference in the brain. Autism is, at the time of writing, considered to affect about 1% of the population but it could potentially be much higher for reasons I will explain in the more detailed look at Autism in section 3.

Early identification and intervention will often help an individual to cope with life, be happy, understand themself and to understand the world around them. If you suspect a child that you work with may be Autistic but has not yet been diagnosed, speak to your SENCO and see what their thoughts are.

Some Autistic children have good verbal skills and can be highly articulate; these have traditionally been referred to as *higher functioning Autistic*. Some Autistic children have limited or no verbal communication skills; these have traditionally been referred to as *lower functioning Autistic*. These children may rely on communication methods such as Makaton and may additionally sometimes have personal care needs.

General advice

The following are very condensed general guidelines for working with Autistic children. I would like to labour the point for those reading that *every child is different* and all of these may not apply to every Autistic child, but I have found the following to be the best general advice that I can give to anyone about to work with an Autistic child.

- Get to know the child.
- Learn what the child's routine is and stick to it as much as possible as disruption to routine can cause anxiety which can manifest in undesirable ways.
- Establish a personal routine with them. Many autistic children find a predictable routine calming.
- When speaking to them, be direct and to the point.
- When speaking to them avoid metaphors and similes, i.e. *'it is raining cats and dogs'* or *'You are as happy as Larry today'.* They may misunderstand you or simply have no idea what you mean.
- Avoid sarcasm.
- If the child can become aggressive or dysregulated, learn what their triggers are and learn what it looks like when they are getting agitated - reflect on what you are doing and modify your approach as required.
- Beware sensory overload. As far as possible, a minimal environment is generally good. A calm environment is ideal.An environment without multiple people speaking at the same time is good. If the child is in a mainstream school, this can be tricky, but consider the 'least busy' part of the classroom for them. Note, this is *not automatically the back of the classroom*.
- If the child has a strong personal interest (that is school appropriate), encourage them to decorate their working space with some pictures of this

- Incorporate the child's interests into learning and interaction where possible.
- Autistic children are sometimes good at memorising things (Rote learning). This can be used to get a child to memorise words, facts and figures that can then be contextualised in a lesson around that subject.
- Social norms can be difficult for some Autistic children to understand. Model prosocial behaviour and discuss with the child why you are behaving in a particular way and also highlight how actions can make others feel.
- Social interaction can be challenging for many Autistic children. Be aware of this and support them, as appropriate, in their interactions with their peers. Some Autistic children will be good at making friends, playing and interacting - these will need less support in this area. Some Autistic children will struggle with basic social interaction and maintaining friendships. See if there is a strategy in place for supporting them in this. If there is not, you may have to take the lead.

Strategies and adaptations

A great strategy to try out with some Autistic children are some visual aids to communication around mood and feelings.

For example, you could use some mood faces. These are especially well suited to younger children but will work with some older children too.

> These are a series of faces showing different moods such as, happy, sad, silly, proud, angry, excited, worried/anxious, tired, scared etc. There are usually many variations of this available online for free.

If the child has communication difficulties, or is not always inclined to talk freely, they can indicate their mood by placing something on the appropriate face to communicate how they are feeling or that they require reassurance, for example.

Some children may benefit from a simpler scale to convey how they are feeling. This could be a scale from *1 to 5* or *1 to 10,* as the child prefers. This could be smiley faces going from saddest / angriest (1) to happiest (5). The child can then indicate how they are feeling at any given time by pointing to their scale, or they can place a preferred object on the scale to indicate.

Scales such as these can be customised for the individual child. Some may prefer:
- Numbers
- Descriptions
- Smiley faces
- A gradient from one colour to another (i.e. Red to Green)
- Characters from a film
- Something else that is meaningful to them and can be understood by any adult that is briefed on the meaning of the scale.

Please refer to the **standard classroom adaptation**, if you are teaching, for how to make your lessons as accessible as possible to as many children as possible, including Autistic Spectrum Condition kids.

2.3 Depression

Depression can affect any of us at any point in our lives. The chances are that most of the people reading this will have at least some personal experience of depression, either in their own lives at some point or of someone that they know.

Depression can occur in children and teenagers quite easily and should be taken seriously as it can potentially progress onto behaviours such as *self-harming* and *eating disorders* (covered shortly).

Depression can be caused by a variety of different things (or combinations of things) that can happen in a child or teens life. For example,
- Issues at home or with a specific family member.
- Being the victim of bullying at home, in school or outside of school.
- Not feeling understood or listened to.
- Ongoing abuse or past trauma.
- The onset of other mental health difficulties.
- Having a negative self-image and comparing themselves unfavourably to other people or media images.
- Bereavement. Death of a friend or family member.
- Divorce of parents.

Whatever the cause may be, it is important that you should have a sense of curiosity about the causes of the child's depression. In some cases, it may be fairly obvious what is causing the depression, for example they have been taken into care or a family member may have died. In other cases it may be more difficult to determine what the causes of depression are, unless you are directly told.

It is possible that the cause of their depression, if definitely known by you, may seem minor in your view, but it is important to remember that we all have different levels of resilience and a negative life event can be relative in its impact, i.e. what one person might shrug off, another might find extremely traumatic.

I was personally plunged into a depression by the untimely death of a well-loved cat who I had looked after from the time of their birth. I had taken their mother in, who was a starving, pregnant, stray cat who appeared in my back garden one day looking for food and shelter.

This story might evoke in some, *'it was only a cat'* and it might seem like something that is not such a big deal, but to me it was a cause of great sadness and caused me depression. So, try to remember, life events affect different people in different ways and your perception of their seriousness is very unimportant compared to the impact that it has on the individual who is suffering from depression for whatever reason.

What you know about a child could just be the tip of the iceberg, so maintain your sense of curiosity about what is happening for the child who you identify as being depressed or are informed is suffering from depression.

Some signs of depression can include but are not limited to:

- Withdrawal from social interaction with peers or friends or wanting to spend long periods on their own without interacting.
- Sadness or a low mood that does not seem to go away of its own accord.
- Irritability and sometimes unexpected anger.
- A lack of interest in things in general, or a lack of interest in things which they might usually have enjoyed.
- Tears which may *seem* unrelated to external stimuli around them.
- They may seem tired or exhausted a lot of the time or lack energy to do much.
- They may have difficulty sleeping or maintaining a regular sleeping pattern.
- They may seem to lose interest in eating food or they may seem to eat excessively.
- They may gain or lose weight (please see separate section on *eating disorders*).
- They may speak negatively of themself, describing themself as worthless, useless or they may verbalise that there is no point in existence or things in general.
- They may verbalise having suicidal thoughts or begin to take an interest in researching methods of suicide on the internet.
- They may begin to self harm or there may be evidence of self harming. Please see the separate section on self harm.

As with most of the things I discuss in this book:

Early intervention is massively important.

If you suspect that a child is suffering from depression this should be reported immediately to your school's SENCO and management. Hopefully they will take it seriously and will have something in place to support the child through what can be an extremely difficult time in their childhood.

Unfortunately it is a fact that in sometimes underfunded schools with staff who have unreasonably heavy workloads, children can fall through the gaps and not receive the support that they need. This is a sad fact but it is a reality that many of us will be aware of. What can we individually do if this is the case?

The family

If you are able to contact the family, fosterer or carer and it is appropriate to do so, it may be worth delicately broaching the subject with them. You could potentially start the conversation about something positive that the child has done at school and then move on to their well-being as an important discussion point. You may find that the parent/carer has equal concerns but does not know what to do or you may find that they were completely unaware there is a problem. This is surprisingly common.

Some parents can be in a complete state of denial about their children and it is important to acknowledge this. A solid example of this is a young person who was in care, who I worked with many years ago. They were a nice kid, and I got along with them well.

They were known to have bouts of depression and did have a therapist who was appointed to help them with this.

This particular kid was allowed to have contact with their family (which I regarded as being a fairly dysfunctional family if I am honest).

The child in question had recently been informed that the entire family, all of the siblings and aunties and uncles etc, would be going on an exciting two week holiday in Europe together. The only thing was that their child who was in care was not invited. The family informed them of this in a very matter of fact way.

Unsurprisingly the child lapsed into quite a deep depression at this further rejection by their parents and family. They became unresponsive and withdrawn and struggled to get out of bed for school, which they usually enjoyed a great deal. I was growing increasingly concerned for the poor child.

Interestingly, during telephone interactions with the child, the grandmother and mother had noticed that she seemed particularly depressed and withdrawn.

Even more interestingly, they arrived at the conclusion that their child's sudden depression was likely due to something that was happening at school or in the care home.

I had a particularly awkward conversation with the grandmother and mother where I had to point out the actual source of depression for this poor kid.

What might seem completely obvious to most readers, came as a complete revelation to the family, that it was actually their action of deliberately excluding the child from a family holiday which everyone else was invited on. There was a long and difficult silence whilst they processed this uncomfortable truth. They never really forgave me for pointing this out to them but it was in the child's best interests to be honest with their family. The child remained with us whilst the family holidayed and we did our best to rally their spirits and distract them.

The reason I share this sad story is to highlight the fact that some parents can spectacularly lack insight around the impact that their own behaviour and actions can have on their children. This is something to be aware of when interacting with families.

Some parents can do everything right in being supportive and considerate around their children and the child may still suffer from depression. Either way, it is often worth having a conversation with the family unless you have specifically been told not to by your SENCO or head teacher. You can always ask first.

The family may be able to get their GP to make a referral to an organisation such as CAMHS (Child and Adolescent Mental Health Service). Whilst there can be long waiting lists for CAMHS, due to the inadequate levels of government funding currently provided for them, CAMHS can provide things like counselling, CBT (cognitive Behavioural Therapy) and various other therapies.

Your school may even have a counsellor attached to it and a budget of providing sessions for children at the school. This is useful if they do, but it is not guaranteed.

You may have a *pastoral lead* or a similarly designated person who is tasked with looking after the wellbeing of the children. If you have such an appointed person, speak to them about what support may be available or what strategies they may have in place to use with children suffering from depression.

What can I do myself?

Talking and listening

Talking can be of key importance in tackling depression. Encourage the child to talk to you about things, large or small, that may be bothering them or to talk about what is going on in their life right now. Make time for them and actually listen to them. As stated previously, their woes may seem minor to you, but it is all relative and all of us have different levels of resilience.

The child may or may not want to talk to you about their private thoughts, but it is important that you are clear that you are available if they do want to talk about anything. Having an existing positive relationship with the child can be useful in this.

It is important that we use our active listening skills if the child is talking to us about something that is bothering them. Active listening is usually defined by the five points that follow:
- Pay attention to them. Give them your undivided attention and acknowledge what they are saying.
- Show that you are listening to them.
- Give them feedback.

- Do not pass judgement on what they are saying (although it may need to be discussed with the DSL).
- Respond to them appropriately.

Use active listening as appropriate to the individual child. It is important that they know that you are listening and this can be achieved via a number of ways in practice.
- Making periodic eye contact.
- Making remarks like 'I understand'.
- Nodding your head in acknowledgement.
- Not being on your phone or laptop whilst they are talking to you.
- Letting them speak without interrupting them unless you need to clarify something they have said.

Active listening is a valuable way to make a child feel heard and cared about.

The emotional check in

Earlier in the book I described the emotional check. The child may not want to talk to you, but you can make it clear that you do care and are interested in their well being by doing an emotional check in when they arrive in your class or school. You can simply ask them how things are going. You may receive quite a rude or blunt response, but you are the adult and you should be able to assimilate that in the scheme of things.

Don't be judgemental

Accept what the child is telling you as their legitimate feelings. Do not under any circumstances tell the child to *emself together', 'get over it', 'you shouldn't really be bothered about that'* etc, or suggest that they are attention seeking. These are not helpful statements to make.

The phrase *'Attention Seeking'* should really be struck from your vocabulary when working with children who have depression and similar difficulties.

2.4 Self harm

The following section may be triggering for some people who have experience of self-harm.

Self-harm can occur in children and teenagers for a variety of reasons and is not always simple to understand. The reasons behind it can be complex. The physical pain of the act of self-harming can sometimes distract from the emotional pain and turmoil that may be happening for that individual, however this is not always the case.

Hopefully if a child is a known self-harmer, they have already been referred for appropriate help and support from a qualified professional and there will be a support strategy in place for staff to follow, but this is not automatically the case. So, if you have reason to suspect that a child is self-harming, refer it to the SENCO or your line manager immediately and do not be shy in asking them for progress updates with what is happening in terms of a referral or appropriate support - make sure that the wheels are turning. This is an appropriate thing for you to check up on.

Some of the warning signs that a child may be self-harming (if they have not made a disclosure to you directly) are as follows, so keep an eye out for these.
- If a child has been cutting themselves, they may wear long sleeves all of the time, even when the weather is very hot and it is inappropriate attire. This can potentially be to cover up marks that are left by the act of self-harming.

- You may see blood on their clothing or possibly tissues with blood on them which have been used to clean up after an act of self-harm.
- You may see unexplained bruises, bites, cut marks etc on their body.
- They may become withdrawn from their peers or choose to spend a lot of their time alone. Their interaction may change with staff and their peers. They may start to avoid interaction all together with people who they would usually interact with.
- They may exhibit 'risky behaviours' including drugs and alcohol consumption if they have access to these. It is important to report this if you see an interest in drugs developing so that someone (such as your SENCO or line manager) can refer them and offer support.
- They may exhibit mood swings that are unusual for them or have uncharacteristic outbursts.

The list above is not exhaustive and in isolation any of these potential warning signs can be explained by other things, but if you have suspicions, do not under any circumstances keep them to yourself. Any suspicions around a child beginning to self-harm must be reported immediately. The consequences for not doing so can be as extreme as a child attempting suicide and potentially succeeding in this.

There can be many causes for self-harming in teenagers and children; some of the causes that occur with some frequency are as follows:
- This can be a response to past trauma or ongoing trauma or abuse.

- They may be attempting to cope with depression, anxiety problems or it may accompany an eating disorder which has developed or is developing.
- They may have problems within their family or within their care home which may need further investigation by an appropriately trained person.
- They may be grieving after a bereavement and require referral for counselling.
- They may be actively being bullied either in school or outside of school. If this is happening, it is essential that steps are taken to resolve the situation and that it is reported to the appropriate person, probably your line manager.
- They could potentially have other mental health problems which could be developing which they are attempting to cope with via self-harm. If this is the case they may need to be referred for some kind of therapy so that they can learn a better coping mechanism.
- It could be caused by memories from earlier incidents of abuse/neglect/trauma surfacing and under these circumstances it can be an attempt to cope with what are very painful memories to process.
- The child may have low self-esteem or a negative body image which causes them to self-harm. There are structured exercises that can be done around self-esteem for young people.

The above list is not exhaustive but gives you some ideas around what the causes can potentially be.

If there is already a plan in place at your school to support a child who is a known self-harmer, please learn the contents of that plan and follow it. Do not feel unable to critique it or challenge it. If you are of the opinion that something on a plan is not appropriate or even not helpful, contact the appropriate person and explain your concern to them. They may agree with you, they may not. It is good to do this via email so that you can compose your thoughts and you have a record of the concern that you have raised.

Never under any circumstances tell a child that they are 'attention seeking' if they self-harm. Do not frame a child's behaviour like this when you discuss it with colleagues under any circumstances. If a colleague refers to a child's self-harming as *'attention seeking behaviour'*, you should challenge them over this as it is extremely unhelpful and negative.

The child deserves our attention and support and it is a part of our job. If colleagues in school or residential care persist in referring to self-harm as *'attention seeking behaviour'*, they should be referred to the DSL (designated safeguarding lead) and the head of school as this is a serious issue in my opinion.

If there is not a plan in place to support a child who is self-harming, there are some general guidelines that you can follow. I will list some of these here but please be aware that these are not universal.

- Be there for them. Let the child know that if they want to talk, you are available and happy to listen, without judgement. Of course the contents of the discussion may not be able to remain confidential if there are things which must be reported to the DSL or manager and you would indicate this to the child as required. Let them know that it is ok for them to

be honest and open with you and that you are not standing in judgement on what they tell you, however difficult it may be for you to hear.
- If a child discloses something that you find too emotionally distressing to deal with, talk to your DSL and line manager immediately.
- Stay calm. Take a deep breath and focus on the child. It can be highly distressing to see a child harm themselves or talk about suicide, but we may potentially be the only adult they are comfortable to disclose to and discuss what they are going through. Even though it can be challenging, you may have to try and be that child's rock if you can.
- Try and focus on what is causing the self-harm rather than the act of self-harm itself. Try to explore what the problems are and try to be proactive in finding ways to resolve things that are causing the child distress.
- If a child trusts you, you may be able to ask them to simply come to you without judgement if they self-harm so that you can offer first aid (if you are appropriately trained to do so) or take them to a first aider so that they can receive treatment.
- Stripping down an environment for a child so that they will find it difficult to self-harm can make for a completely empty room resembling a cell. This is a profoundly negative way to approach the problem. We follow common sense rules like not leaving craft knives, scissors or tools laying around, but it will not help a child if we put them in a bare room, this is not a therapeutic approach in an educational setting.
- If a child is determined to find a way to self-harm, they will usually be able to. For example, I have

known some children who whilst on trips out of the school grounds have scanned the floor for broken pieces of glass and then concealed these in their trainers. Whilst we must always be extremely vigilant for risk to the child, the solution to the problem may more often lay in meeting the child's emotional needs.

In many cases where there is not yet CAMHS (Child and Adolescent Mental Health Services) or other medical professionals involved, there are various strategies that you can attempt with a child. It is very important that if CAMHS are involved and they have drawn up a plan of strategies for the child that you follow that plan rather than improvising. If there is no support or plan in place you may have to improvise and try to do what you can to support the child through their dark night.

The following are some strategies that may be potentially helpful for the child. Every child is different and there is unfortunately no magic wand when it comes to self-harm, but we in education may be able to do something whilst the child is on a waiting list, as can happen all too often.

Please note that *distraction* is a key concept in many of the following strategies that I suggest. You may develop other ways of distracting a child that are tailored to their personality or quirks and that is fine.

Particularly violent methods of distraction should be discouraged. For example, I once discovered that an inexperienced teaching assistant had developed a coping strategy with a child who was suffering from some trauma related depression, which involved violently acting out and stabbing cardboard boxes with a pair of scissors and shouting.

This type of strategy is extremely inappropriate. I spoke to the teaching assistant and told her that she would have to use some different strategies in helping the child to cope as stabbing was not appropriate behaviour to practise and learn. She was not happy with this, but teaching a child to cope like this is not ok. The following are a bit more productive and useful.

The glitter bottle

Not every child will go for this but I have found it to work very well in some cases. The child is given a *plastic* bottle with a generous amount of glitter in it and filled with water. The child is encouraged to carry this around with them, or to have it at their desk or in their booth.

When the child has thoughts about self-harm, they are encouraged to shake the glitter bottle up and then set it down on the desk. They are encouraged to focus on watching the glitter settle in the bottle and reflect on this before they attempt anything further.

Some children and teens find this therapeutic and find that it can help divert them from sometimes obsessing thoughts.

Writing distraction

The child can be encouraged to write down all of their problems or the things that are currently making them unhappy on a sheet of paper. As part of the exercise the child is then encouraged to tear the paper up, shred it, screw it into a ball and dispose of it.

This is a symbolic act that some children will gain some relief from by symbolically destroying the things that are distressing them.

Some children will gain relief from doodling or scribbling in red ink on a paper. If a child wants to do this as a form of distraction, it should be allowed as it is a more healthy form of venting than actual self-harming.

Sensory distractions

Some children may find a more sensory approach to be appropriate to their needs. There are a couple of commonly found methods for this which includes the following.

When a child has identified that they are becoming unsettled or having thoughts of self-harm, one strategy that they can use is to be given an ice cube which they hold in their hand until it has completely melted. Some children find this a therapeutic way to distract themself from thoughts of active self-harm.

Other children may prefer to have an elastic band loose around their wrist. This must be very carefully done so that there is no risk of them cutting off their circulation or using it as a tourniquet. In order to minimise the risk of a child using something as a tourniquet, you should have some appropriate scissors easily available to staff for cutting a tourniquet. These are easily available online.

When the child starts to have thoughts about self harm they can ping themselves on the wrist with the elastic band as a substitute for actual self-harming.

As strange as this may sound, this can actually be a legitimate coping strategy for some self-harmers that helps them to stop short of actual self-harm.

Further distraction

Another method of distraction for the struggling child or teen can be listening to some music. This *should* ideally be upbeat or energetic music. Some perfectly good music is very downbeat in its lyrical content but can contribute very negatively to mood. I can remember listening to some particularly gloomy and angsty music as a teen which really did nothing to help me through low moods.

Do not be judgemental or allow your personal prejudices about genre to dictate the kind of music a child is allowed to put on their headphones. I recall one member of staff categorically stating that a teenage child was not allowed to listen to Jungle/dancehall as a means of distraction. I asked the teacher why they had decreed this. They responded that they think Jungle is a horrible noise. Not a valid reason. The child actually had some pretty good mixtapes and it was entirely appropriate for them to distract themself with this. It is more problematic if the lyrical content is fixated on subjects like loss and suicide; then they should be potentially steered elsewhere.

It may be appropriate in some settings for a child to be allowed to watch something. Think sitcoms, cartoons, comedy films. Something that will lighten their mood. In the unlikely event they want to watch a film with troubling themes such as the Czechoslovakian new wave film *'the cremator'*, they should probably save that for some other time and place.

Equally some children may find refuge in reading novels (or even factual books) This should be actively encouraged as a method of self-diversion, although some attention should be paid to the reading material. One girl I worked with for a couple years had a habit of reading particularly tear jerking fictions based around tragedy and abuse.

After devouring yet another of these cheap novels which a member of care home staff had supplied them with in the belief that it might help them to process their own trauma, there would inevitably be a period of self-harming. I suggested that we work to introduce her to more life affirming and age appropriate works of fiction.

It is always worth keeping a curious eye on the type of media which the child is consuming. Please leave your personal prejudices out of it though. If the kid likes heavy metal or drum and bass and it is not your jam, don't be judgemental. If the kid likes LGBTQ+ teen fiction, do not judge or speculate that this genre may feed into their self-harm. This would be a profoundly negative, out dated and unacceptable line of reasoning - please educate yourself on equality, diversity and Inclusion.

> *"Think for yourselves and let others enjoy the privilege to do so, too."*
> Voltaire

Physical distractions

Some young people may find physical activities useful in diverting themselves from troubling thoughts that they may have difficult in managing.

Some young people may find the following useful depending on their personality and interests:
- A vigorous round with a punch bag to release their negative feelings.
- A run. Some young people (and adults) find the physical act of running to be calming and to help them cope with troubling thoughts and impulses.
- Yoga. I am an advocate of Yoga for children as it is generally a positive activity that can have a range of benefits for the individual. If the child has at some point learned some Yoga and they find this useful, ask your manager to dust off their purse and get them a Yoga mat to do this on if it helps them.
- At the end of the day, if the strategy you develop with a child is within reason, then go with it. If they do 20 star jumps to help themself cope with a difficult moment, then that is a lot better than self-harming

Getting the child to talk will probably remain as my preferred strategy with children who self-harm. Many kids have responded to a therapeutic approach and some kind words and simply being there to listen to them. Many kids have opened up to me simply because I was there for them and had taken the time to get to know them a bit and this has often been a very useful thing for them.

Not every child will engage in therapy and some will be particularly resistant to engaging in it. If the only person they will talk to is a teaching assistant, the Art teacher, the cleaner or anyone else then build on that as a potential way for the child to access some kind of support.

Also, importantly, make your classroom a safe haven, somewhere a kid who is going through a tough time actively wants to be. Make the activities fun and meaningful and if you work in a school with smaller classes such as an SEN school, feel free to throw in some extra activities that they enjoy, if not to the detriment of the other children in the class.

2.5 Eating disorders

The contents of this section could be potentially triggering for some people, so please be aware of support which is available to you if you may be upset by the discussion of eating disorders.

This section on eating disorders is deliberately placed next to the section on self-harm as there can be some overlap between these two things. I have worked with a significant number of young people who have a mixture of self-harm, eating disorders and depression.

So what is an eating disorder? This is when someone's relationship to eating and food is atypical. This kind of disorder can affect a child or teenager's eating habits in a negative way and can also carry a component of self-image problems. For example, their sense of an ideal body could have been profoundly influenced by Photoshopped images of people to aspire to in the mainstream media.

Their eating habits, behaviours and attitudes towards food can become highly problematic and further mental health problems can develop. If the eating disorder progresses unchecked, it can cause physical health issues which can become very serious. Eating disorders can often develop when someone is of school age and can especially develop during the teen years. Early intervention is always preferable if possible.

However, some children can slip between the cracks in a school and do not get the help they need early on and so the problem can become more serious. Keep your eyes open and report anything that doesn't seem right to your SENCO and manager.

It is currently estimated that there may be as many as 1.25 million people in the UK with an eating disorder, but it is difficult to quantify the prevalence of a condition that is often secretive in its nature.

Whilst research indicates that eating disorders are more common in girls, it is an important factor to consider that boys can also suffer from an eating disorder, so it is important not to be dismissive of the needs of *any* of the children you are working with.

There are 4 varieties of eating disorder that you are most likely to come across in your career. I will give a very brief summary of these for you. Remember, if you suspect a child has an eating disorder, it is not your job to diagnose them (unless you are qualified to do so of course) but it is your job to report and support. The 4 main varieties that we will look at are Anorexia, Bulimia, binge eating and Restrictive Food Intake Disorder (RFID).

Anorexia

Typically, people with Anorexia will do some of the following:
- Have a very restricted diet and eat very small amounts of food, sometimes obsessively weighing the amounts that they eat and calculating the calorie intake. Often there will be an ideal calorie intake that is desired by the Anorexic; this will usually be well below the recommended level.

- Have a heightened or pervasive fear of gaining any weight.
- In addition to having a fear of gaining weight, they may also have a distorted sense of body image. For example, when they look at themself in a mirror they may perceive themself as being a completely different shape to that which they are, and may have extremely negative thoughts about their own appearance resulting in further food restriction and a further impact upon their health.
- They may do fasts and exercise excessively.
- They may use high levels of laxatives in order to try and not gain weight from that which they eat.
- It has sometimes been known for anorexics to use amphetamines for their appetite suppressant qualities. Obviously Amphetamines are addictive and can cause additional problems like psychosis and mood swings if used to excess.

Anorexia can have a serious impact on the health of the children that you work with but it is worth remembering that adults can also be affected by any of the eating disorders that are listed here.

Some of the main health threats that can arise because of Anorexia are as follows:

- Heart problems - irregular heartbeats and unusually slow heartbeats.
- Irregular periods or even a cessation of their periods.
- Depression, Anxiety and self-harming.
- Low blood pressure and the problems that can be caused by this.

- Weak bones and being prone to fractures/breaks.
- Feelings of weakness, dizziness and fainting.
- Bloating, constipation and other digestive problems.

Bulimia

Typically, people with Bulimia will do some of the following:

- They will often overeat and may feel completely out of control to stop eating. This is mostly referred to as *binge eating.*
- After binge eating they may feel intense emotions of self-disgust or remorse. This is not universal.
- After binge eating the Bulimic will usually do something that they consider to be compensation for their binge. These are often things like:
    - Deliberately making themself sick after eating. This is called purging and it is usually done in secret.
    - Use excessive amounts of laxatives, weight loss pills or amphetamines.
    - Exercise excessively. This can happen to the point of causing physical issues.
- People with Bulimia will often judge themselves or their worth as a person by their weight and body shape. Failure to hit sometimes highly unrealistic targets for weight may result in depression, despair and anxiety.

Some of the main health risks associated with Bulimia are as follows:

- Irregular heartbeats.

- Blood in the stools or vomit.
- Tooth decay and cavities (caused by exposure to stomach acids).
- Swollen cheeks due to their salivary glands being stressed.
- Persistent tiredness, dizziness and fainting.
- Self-harming.

Binge eating

Typically, someone who is a binge eater will do the following:

- Eat large amounts of food even if they are not hungry
- They will frequently over eat and will often feel powerless to stop themself from overeating
- They will often gain weight and may have health concerns associated with obesity
- They may suffer emotional distress after binge eating, such as feelings of guilt, remorse and worthlessness

Some of the main health risks associated with binge eating are:

- High blood pressure (which can ultimately lead to heart disease or a stroke).
- Sleep apnoea (breathing stopping and starting during sleep).
- Diabetes.
- Fatty liver.

Avoidant/ Restrictive Food Intake Disorder (ARFID)

Some research has shown that ARFID and Autism can occur together. Some research suggests that as many as a third of people with ARFID can also be Autistic which is a significant statistic. So, in practice there can be some overlap of these two conditions.

When someone has two conditions at the same time, it is called a *comorbidity*. The two conditions can interact in various complex ways.

There can also be a *comorbidity* between ARFID and Obsessive Compulsive Disorder (OCD) and Anxiety Disorder.

People with ARFID may typically have some of the following symptoms:
- They are disinterested in food.
- They may find the texture, smell, colour, appearance of all foods off putting or may find this with many types of food.
- They will often lose weight or be below the expected weight for their age.
- They are not usually afraid of gaining weight.
- They do not usually have a poor body image as part of this condition.

Some of the health risks posed by ARFID are as follows:
- To not get enough of the vitamins and other substances that are essential to a healthy body.

- They may have stunted growth due to their poor diet and may not grow to their potential height.

Some warning signs to be aware of

It is part of our job as conscientious professionals who work with kids to be aware of the warning signs that an eating disorder might be developing in a child.

The following are potential signs that one of the young people that you work with may have an eating disorder or may potentially be developing one. This is split into *physical symptoms*, i.e. those that you may detect in their appearance or relating to their body and physical health and *emotional symptoms,* i.e., those which you may detect as a variance in their wellbeing or behaviours.

Physical symptoms
- Someone with Anorexia will typically be very thin and may present as having very little body fat. Conversely, someone with Bulimia can be of any body shape or size.
- You may see some unusual swelling of the salivary glands. These are to be found to the sides of the face, on the jawline, starting from the ears downward. These may be painful or very tender.
- Their period may become irregular or cease.
- Their weight may fluctuate, i.e. rapid weight gain and loss.
- They may feel cold all of the time even in good weather/ warm rooms.
- They can develop fine hair over the body which would usually be absent.

- They may experience gastrointestinal cramps on a regular basis (pains in the stomach and intestines).
- Wounds may take an unusually long time to heal.
- The immune system may be compromised, resulting in persistent colds and regularly being very ill.
- Sleep problems, difficulty concentrating, fainting, dizziness and lethargy.

Emotional Symptoms
- They may be preoccupied with the calorie content of food.
- They may seem preoccupied with their weight and/or figure.
- They may be preoccupied or obsessed with dieting.
- They may have a very negative view of their own physical appearance or may have unrealistic expectations/ goals of their own weight/ appearance.
- They may be uncomfortable eating around others or refuse to eat if other people are present.
- They may regularly exit directly after eating to go to the bathroom. This may be to *purge*, i.e. to make themself sick.
- Ritualised behaviour around food. Only eating one food type at a time, or only eating, for example, ketchup or some other unusual main food. Not allowing different foods to touch on their plate.
- Depression.
- Anxiety.
- Self-harming.

If you are working with a child or teenager who you think may be developing an eating disorder or who may already have one, it is imperative that you pass this information on to the SENCO and the management of your school. Hopefully they will have a strategy for how to support the child.

However this is not always the case. You may find yourself in a situation where you are not supported in your school the way that you should be. If you find yourself in this position, there are various help lines that you can contact for confidential advice about how you can support the child. Use a search engine to locate some current ones.

It is also worth noting that Vegetarianism and Veganism are not signs that a child could have an eating disorder. These are relevant and valid lifestyle/ dietary choices that an individual can make at any point in their life. It is also a myth that children need to consume meat to have a healthy diet and to grow properly. If a child has made legitimate lifestyle choices that are different to yours, you should respect this and not try to make them conform to what you regard as the norm.

Of course, a child who is Vegan or Vegetarian can have an eating disorder but these things are not by default linked outside of the feverish imaginations of some individuals who have an issue with diversity in dietary choices.

Strategies and adaptations

So, how might we support and help children in the area of eating disorders?

I am a firm believer that we should be proactive in our approach to what can be a terrible thing for a child to cope with, and that we should take a structured approach to doing work with all of the children that we work with on eating disorders to raise awareness.

This should be age appropriate. Your school might already have a strategy to tackle this, but sometimes a school's approach is not very robust and can simply pay lip service to an issue that affects young people in a very serious way rather than really tackle it.

If you find that your school's approach is lacking, see what you can do to encourage the powers that be to take more of an interest, and at the very least, you should do some work with the children that you directly work with.

At a girl's residential school which I used to work at, I used to do some workshops around media representations of women, including how Photoshop is used to achieve unrealistic standards of appearance. I would initiate discussions on how this could cause issues for young people in terms of their relationship with their own body and appearance. This is easier to do than you may think.

I would also do some work around the physical effects that eating disorders can have on the body. You have this information a few pages back that you can use to inform a workshop for your learners to participate in.

I also used to do a quiz at the end of the session, where one of the questions would be what the number for an appropriate helpline for advice about eating disorders was. This would be left on the board and the learners would be allowed to copy it down from the board to score a point (and in case they needed it).

There are a few documentaries that can potentially be screened for your learners to watch as part of a lesson. One such documentary is called *'Miss Representation'*. Whilst I do not unreservedly recommend this documentary, it is a useful thing to show to perhaps teenage learners as it is accessible to younger viewers. This focuses on media representations of women and the detrimental effect that this can have on young people in terms of their self-image and psychological well-being.

I have had good results from showing this to groups of learners and having discussion groups afterwards. This has previously served as an access point to broader discussion around eating disorders. You have to remember that yours may be the only positive voice in the child's life on such subjects and so it is important to tackle such things in a constructive and accessible fashion.

Be warned however; as I recall there is one use of the *'F bomb'* during the documentary, so if that is going to get you sacked, then you had best skip over that particular interview.

Support we can give

It is important to offer your support to a child with an eating disorder. You can acknowledge to them that you know what they are going through and that you are there to help and support them.

Try to talk to them about it and listen to what they have to say. Talking about the problem is an important part of their recovery. If they do not want to talk about it, do not push too hard, but also do not drop the subject completely.

Remain calm. Most of us care about the children we work with and so it can be emotionally taxing to hear them talk about their eating disorder or self-harming. It is important that you remain calm and non-judgemental when discussing it with them or this can have a negative effect on the child.

Do not blame or judge them. Under no circumstances challenge them with things like 'how would this make your mum feel?' or similar tactics which could induce feelings of guilt or shame. This would be a classic example of how to do things really badly. Instead, focus on getting them to share how they are feeling and listen to them.

Generally speaking you should avoid talking about their appearance, even if you are attempting to pay them a compliment. This may set off negative thoughts about themself and cause them to dwell on their own negative self-image.

Try to find constructive ways for them to distract themself and find activities which they can gain some enjoyment from.

I worked with a young lady many years ago, who was a really great kid and used to light up the room when she was in a good space emotionally. She suffered from a quite severe eating disorder and after discussion, we agreed that I would teach her to play guitar (as a distraction for her and also something positive to be doing in her spare time).

We would regularly meet up at school at designated times and pick up our guitars. For some reason that I now forget, I had initially chosen to teach her an old surf guitar instrumental song from the early 60s, but she was happy with that perhaps unusual choice.

The guitar lessons were also a valuable space where she could talk about anything that was on her mind and just generally vent if she felt like it. This was actually quite a useful space for her as the support in most of the other areas of her life was fairly poor.

She never really mastered the guitar, but she practised and always used to turn up. The point is, that the sessions were designed to be therapeutic in nature and gave her a safe space to discuss anything that she wanted to, as well as learn an instrument, which was largely incidental.

The activity that you do with a child can be based on whatever they are interested in. Some kids participate in board games, dungeons and dragons, arts and crafts, sports, whatever it is, you can use sessions of their preferred activity as a way of offering support and distraction.

Importantly ask them what you can do to support them. They may have some good ideas of their own.

Ultimately, a child with an eating disorder will most likely need professional help; it is unlikely that you alone will be able to cure them. Professional help can be a long time coming sometimes - this is a fact unfortunately. So if you find yourself in a position where a child is on a waiting list for support, you now have some strategies that you can try and use to support them through what can be an incredibly tough time.

2.6 ODD (Oppositional Defiant Disorder)

Oppositional Defiant Disorder (or ODD) is a condition that affects some children in such a way as they may behave in a hostile manner to those around them on a consistent basis. We will look more at the details of this shortly.

ODD is thought to have a very common comorbidity with ADHD. It is thought that around half of children with ADHD also have ODD. So if you work with a child who is diagnosed with ADHD, it is possible that they may also have ODD. You can ask if this has been assessed.

As we currently understand it, ODD is more common in boys than girls. The condition usually starts to manifest in the preschool years where a child may appear to have more tantrums and display more negative behaviours than is generally considered normal. Without *proper intervention*, the behaviour will usually continue as they get older.

The causes of ODD are not well understood at the time of writing, but it is thought to be likely that it is caused by either, or a mixture of

- Genetics. There could be something different in the way that the brain of the child functions which gives rise to the behaviours that we associate with ODD. In this respect it is potentially similar to ADHD.
- Environment. There could be some issue with the parenting which the child receives. For example, there could be pervasive factors at play such as a lack of supervision or boundaries around their

behaviour, inconsistent or excessively harsh discipline or even neglect and abuse.

So we can see that either *nature* or *nurture* may potentially give a child the disposition to behave in the way that we call ODD. If a child has learnt behaviours, these can potentially be unlearnt via therapy. If the condition has a neurological basis, i.e. a difference with their brain, then the condition may possibly be present throughout life, but they may be able to moderate the behaviours with structured support and therapy.

The behaviours that are associated with ODD in a child will usually extend to their family, sometimes their peers, adults in general and very often *authority figures,* such as teachers.

Whilst there is some clear overlap with ADHD, ODD is classed as a separate condition as it has some unique aspects of its own. The hostility that stems from ODD will often consist of at least some of the following components:

Angry/ irritable mood
- They often lose their temper, perhaps over minor things.
- They are often touchy or easily annoyed.
- They are often resentful and/or angry.

Argumentative/ defiant behaviour
- They will often argue with authority figures or adults.
- They will often refuse to comply with instructions given by adults or teachers, sometimes seemingly just for the sake of it.

- They may often seek to deliberately annoy others.
- They may often blame others for their own behaviour or mistakes.

Vindictiveness
- They may engage in vindictive patterns of behaviour, i.e. seeking revenge for perceived injustice.

If a child were to receive a medical diagnosis of ODD, they would usually have to show a few of the above symptoms for at least 6 months. If a child has a few 'off days' where they show some of the above symptoms for a short while or a few days, it may not indicate ODD and could be caused by something completely different.

If it is an identifiable and persistent pattern of behaviour and they do not have a diagnosis of ODD, it could be worth opening a discussion with your SENCO about the possibility of investigating this, in order to open a dialogue and go on the record with your concern.

ODD can be potentially difficult to manage in mainstream schools and if not managed intelligently, can impact the learning of those around them. Some mainstream schools may seek to simply exclude children with these behaviours. Some teaching staff may have little knowledge or understanding of this condition as it is not as much talked about as ADHD, ASC or Dyslexia for example. This can lead some teachers to simply label a child in a negative way.

The life options for a child who has ODD may be restricted if no one puts in the effort to help them. They may turn to substance abuse, increasingly dangerous behaviour, criminal activity or suicide, so it really is essential to strive to help such a child.

Strategies and adaptations

Like any other SEN, there are always some strategies and interventions that we, as individuals can put in place. There is no magic bullet for ODD and no quick fix, but there are certainly a few things that can be done to try and help the child to have a more fulfilling time at school.

If there is an existing plan in place at the school for how staff should handle the child, it is a good idea to follow this in order that you are acting *consistently* with other staff. If you do not understand the plan, ask the SENCO or person who made the plan to explain it. Don't be afraid to ask why individual things are on there, it's ok to ask questions and if it is a sufficiently well thought out and robust plan, the person who wrote it should have no difficulties explaining it to you.

Some schools, unfortunately, will not have thought so far ahead as to create an individual plan for the child and so you will simply have to manage your own classroom in a logical and consistent manner. Use the following suggestions as much as possible in your personal planning in that case.

Be consistent in your own classroom. Apply the rules, sanctions and rewards consistently. A child will be able to know, or to learn, where they stand this way and there is less ambiguity for them to cope with.

It is a very good idea to have the classroom rules posted on the wall. These should be laminated to make them more difficult to tear up (just in case) and in language that the children can understand. All of the children should be reminded of the rules on a regular basis, so that they are fresh in their minds and the ODD child does not feel singled out. If they want them, and are happy for it to be done, the rules could be posted on their desk but perhaps this should not be forced upon them as it may cause more problems than it would solve with some children.

Ensure that the ODD child is very clear on what the consequences are for their actions in the classroom. For example, loss of 5 minutes of break time, loss of 5 minutes of a play activity.

Equally be very clear on what the rewards are for positive behaviour. This could be a phone call home to praise them, or something specific to your school that you do as a reward.

Have a plan in place to manage serious behaviours. It may be that there is a place in the school that they can go to cool down for 15 minutes if they have done something really unacceptable in class or it may be that there is someone employed by the school who can collect them and speak to them before they are reintegrated into the classroom. This will depend on you and your school. It may be that there could be a call home to a parent to explain what has happened.

If it is appropriate to contact the parents, fosterers or carers, then it is an excellent idea to get them onboard and have a friendly chat with them. If the parents are of a friendly disposition towards the school, then you could find out what strategies work at home and try these out (if appropriate) in the classroom. It could be useful to email a report card home to parents/carers to let them know about the day.

The ODD child may find it difficult to make friends and to maintain friendships. They may also have low self esteem or depression. Keep this in mind when you are dealing with them.

The ODD child may find it difficult to accept praise in front of others. If so, attempt to give them feedback away from their peers or in a way that is acceptable to them. The praise that is given to an ODD child, can be for seemingly small things like

- Not shouting out
- Remaining in their seat
- Putting a good effort into a piece of work or even just attempting it
- Being kind to a peer or being polite

Reinforce the positive behaviours that they show!

It can help a lot to have agreed targets set with the ODD child. There could also be some reward element if they meet their target. Target setting is a good thing to do with many children as it gives them a clear area of focus to work toward. For a child who doesn't have behavioural difficulties, a target might be mastering their 8 times table, for an ODD child, their targets may be more oriented around self-moderation in ways that are useful in the classroom.

Remain calm. If the ODD child gets into a heightened state (that's *kicking off* in layperson's terms) then do not react by shouting or getting into a heightened state yourself. Take a deep breath and keep a cool head. This is less likely to make the situation worse. Under no circumstances should you get into an argument with the child. This is not going to get you anywhere.

Recognise the early warning signs. If you are directly interacting with the child in the classroom and they show some warning behaviours which may come before an outburst, if safe to do so, give them some space for a minute and then try again. If they are not harming themself or the people around them, then it is ok to give them some space. Getting in their face will very likely only make things worse.

Learn their triggers. Different things may trigger different children with ODD. Many different things could make them agitated and make them more likely to behave in a problematic way. These could include but are not restricted to:

- Mentions of family or holidays that would usually be enjoyed with the family if the child is in care.
- The sensation of touch from others.
- Getting too much into their personal space.
- It could be certain sounds.
- Being spoken to in a certain way or addressed in a certain way.
- Certain tasks during the day.
- Transitions between activities could unsettle them.

The above are purely suggestions. You will have to get to know your ODD child and learn what their triggers are.

Recognise the early warning signs of agitation. As you get to know the child you may begin to notice a pattern, meaning that they do certain things before they get into a heightened state. These could include but are not limited to
- Clenching their jaws or blinking repeatedly or having a twitch.
- Balling up of the fists.
- Specific movements like stamping their feet.
- Withdrawing from interaction in the classroom.

Discreetly study the child and look for patterns. Knowing their triggers and the early warning signs can prevent problems from arising at all or may have a dramatic impact on the behaviour and well-being of the child.

It may not be possible in every school, but if you can create a corner of the classroom where a child can go to chill out for a few minutes, this could prevent more serious incidents from developing. The corner could have some sensory toys or toy animals (if they are younger), something of interest to the child and appropriate to their age if possible. It could even be decorated with a few pictures of things that they find soothing or are interested in.

As you get to know the child, and especially if they are at a stage in their personal development where they can recognise when they are getting into a heightened state, one of their strategies could be to go to the chill out corner for a few minutes in order to 'reset' themselves.

Hopefully it could be negotiated that they would not stay in the chill out corner all day, but that they should go back to their seat as soon as they had managed to become more calm. Returning to their seat and using the chill out corner can also be rewarded via verbal praise or whatever method is appropriate for the child.

When communicating with the ODD child, avoid making threatening statements or ultimatums like, *'you had better do your maths or you will find yourself in detention'*. This is unlikely to bring positive results. Instead, give the child limited but good *options*.

Instead, the above could be phrased something like *'I can see you're not happy at the moment but it is not acceptable to shout at me. You can go to the chill out corner for five minutes or you can sit outside of the classroom door and I will check in on you in five minutes before we try the maths.'*

Expectations for behaviour are clearly stated whilst acknowledging the child's emotional state. Then the child is given two positive options for them to choose from. The child should then be left to process the choices and to pick one. Of course, the child may do something of their own choosing which is undesirable, but if no effort is made by the adult, there is unlikely to be any positive result.

Last but not least, put in the groundwork for them to have some positive experiences in school with you and to have some basic connection with you. If the ODD child regards you as one of the adults who isn't a drag to interact with, you will find the day a lot easier to manage and they may actually be a lot happier. Generally speaking, if a kid regards you well, they are less likely to be extremely challenging!

2.7 Dyslexia and the dyslexia spectrum

Dyslexia is a developmental learning difficulty. It does not affect the level of intelligence of the person who has dyslexia or a related condition. Someone is either born with Dyslexia or they are not. Something resembling Dyslexia can sometimes be acquired through brain injury or trauma. Dyslexia is not a condition which clears up with age. However, various adaptations can be put in place to help a person with Dyslexia cope with learning.

Dyslexia is considered to be characterised by the following:
- An ongoing difficulty with reading skills
- An ongoing difficulty with writing skills
- Dyslexia may also affect memory and the ability to memorise instructions
- Dyslexia may also affect the abilities around organisational skills

People with a diagnosis of Dyslexia may be very skilled in other areas and may be very academically able, but have specific difficulties..

This does not mean that people with Dyslexia cannot become proficient in the 4 areas listed above with support and appropriate adaptations put in place for them.

One of the important documents about Dyslexia is the *'Rose report'* of 2009. The research summarised in this suggests that around 10% of the UK population are somewhere on the Dyslexia spectrum, meaning that around 1 in 10 people have dyslexia to a greater or lesser extent.

Which brings me neatly onto one of my pet complaints: Given that around one in ten learners are somewhat Dyslexic, it is highly likely that every single teacher has Dyslexic learners and so adaptations in the classroom should be made as standard, in all classes, for all learners. There is no known detrimental effect on non-Dyslexic learners from having Dyslexia friendly adaptations in their classes, so people really need to be making their spaces Dyslexia friendly by default.

See the separate section on dyslexia a bit further into this book, for more in depth information about this and related conditions.

Strategies and adaptations

When working with Dyslexic people or children it is important to remember that no single adaptation is universal. Different things work best for different people. However there are some good practice guidelines that you can follow. Here are some key ones.

- Ideally your school will have a special dyslexia friendly font like 'open Dyslexic' installed on all machines. Use this as your default font, or use it for any Dyslexic learner. It is probably most useful if you use it as your default font for text.

Patrick the cat

An example of the open Dyslexic font

- If you cannot use the open Dyslexic font, use a Sans Serif font. For anyone who hasn't learnt about typography in the past, the serifs are the little decorative bits on the ends of the letters.
- Sans serif fonts include
    - Comic Sans
    - Arial
    - Verdana
    - Tahoma
    - Calibri
- These will seem less jumbled to many Dyslexic learners.
- Use a bullet point list to break tasks down into instructions for a bigger task.
- Leave instructions on display for the learners to refer back to.
- PowerPoint is good for this - you can type instructions on the fly.
- Use a high contrast background and font, such as mustard and black. Different colours work better for different people and some software has accessibility controls so that users can tweak the appearance and colour schemes to best suit them.

2.8 Dyscalculia

Dyscalculia is a specific learning difficulty which has been compared to Dyslexia. One of the key differences is that it is specific to numbers, rather than writing. It is thought that around 5% of the population has this condition.

Children with Dyscalculia may actually be competent in some aspects of maths such as geometry and shape etc. They will however likely struggle significantly with arithmetic and quantities.

The disadvantage caused by this can persist into adult life as many everyday tasks require at least basic arithmetic. Dyscalculia will often be noticed in primary school where it will be observed that a child with Dyscalculia will struggle with some basic maths and will fall behind. Ideally the child will be noticed by the teaching staff and will get some kind of assessment for this and additional support to meet their needs.

There are some signs that a child may have Dyscalculia:
- The child may become anxious when it is time to do maths.
- The child may go to some lengths to avoid maths or games that involve maths.
- The child may have some difficulty recognising mathematical symbols.
- They may experience a delay in learning to count, or may need to use their fingers to count after their peers have developed past this.
- They may struggle to put numbers in order of size.
- Have difficulty in estimating numbers.

As they get older they may have difficulty in things such as
- Working out what change they should have from transactions.
- Counting out coins.
- Remembering anything to do with figures.
- Have difficulty reading clocks.
- They may have difficulty with the concept of *left and right.*

Whilst Dyscalculia can be very difficult for a child, there are thankfully some supports which can be put in place to help them in class

- Allowing them where possible to use physical objects (like tokens or similar) to help them do maths problems.
- Encourage them to verbalise the steps as they work through maths problems.
- Verbally review with the learner what they have previously learnt before attempting to build on it. Ensure that the learning is secure and fresh before going further into the subject.
- Use concrete examples that relate to the real world before attempting more abstract questions.
- Get them to play games with dice and dominos as this may help them to recognise patterns of dots and how these relate to number.
- Avoid plain worksheets where possible.
- Repetition can be a key factor in the child expanding their understanding of maths. Ideally aim for short focused sessions often. Cover the same ground as much as you need to in order for the child to become secure in the content.

- Try, if possible, to provide them with a quiet place to work with as few distractions as possible. This could be helped by putting a screen next to their workspace, not to isolate them from their peers but to give them a space where they can focus.
- Give them fact sheets to refer to, so that they have to memorise less information relating to maths.

2.9 Learning disabilities

A child can be born with Learning disabilities, or they can acquire them through an illness which causes some damage to the brain or via an accident. Sometimes they can be caused by parental alcohol and drug use whilst pregnant such as FASD (Foetal Alcohol Spectrum Disorder).

There is an important distinction to be made here. A *learning disability* is a separate thing to a *learning difference* or *difficulty*. For example, dyslexia and ADHD can be considered to be learning differences. Someone with either of those conditions may learn in a slightly different manner, but they are capable of learning and their intellectual capacity is not limited by their learning difference.

In contrast, someone with a learning disability is usually limited to a certain point of development by their intellectual capacity and so they may struggle to learn things beyond a certain level and may also struggle with everyday activities. This will usually affect them for their entire life. A learning disability can be acquired at any point in a person's life.

The severity of a learning disability can vary. These are usually classified under different headings depending on the severity of the learning disability.

- Mild Learning Disability
- Moderate Learning Disability
- Severe Learning Disability
- Profound and Multiple Learning Disability

For example, someone with a *Mild Learning Disability* may be fairly able; they may be able to attend a mainstream school and may only need significant support in things like applying for jobs, filling in forms or other complex tasks.

At the other end of the scale, someone with a *Profound and Multiple Learning Disability* (PMLD) may significantly struggle to do much unassisted and may require a high level of care for their entire life.

In practice, you are most likely to find yourself working with severe (and PMLD) if you are working in a specialised setting that specifically deals with the needs of those children, young adults and sometimes older people. If you are working in such a school, there should hopefully be good planning for each learner taking their individual needs into account and also people who are responsible for any personal care needs which individual learners may have.

The curriculum that is followed at such a school may seem reminiscent of the primary curriculum and there may also be an emphasis on life skills, especially with teenagers, where there may be an effort made to help them develop the skills that they will need in the world, for example, making themselves basic food or being able to go to the shops and use a shopping list.

Some people will have a specific condition that is accompanied by a learning disability. For example, some people on the Autistic Spectrum can also have a learning disability. People with Downs syndrome will pretty much always have a learning disability to a greater or lesser extent.

Everyone is different. If you find yourself working with a child with a Mild Learning Disability or you suspect that one you are working with may have this, consider the following. Some potential indicators of a Mild Learning Disability include, but are not restricted to
- Poor memory and concentration skills.
- Delayed development in fine motor skills.
- Difficulty in following instructions; getting confused about the order that things should be done in.
- Difficulties in being organised. Losing things a lot.
- Language may develop more slowly and there may be some difficulty in pronouncing new words.
- There may be a general delay in the levels they achieve across their subjects compared to the average for their peers.

There are some things that we can do to support a learner with Mild Learning Difficulties. How much impact this has depends on the degree of their Learning Difficulty. Try the following:
- Allow them extra time to complete tasks.
- Give them differentiated work that allows for their ability and supports their strengths.
- Chunk new activities into small bite sized pieces and let them master these, one step at a time. Try to keep activities in general, *short and focused.*
- Play to their strengths. If they are good at something in particular, you could include this as a starter activity in order to build their sense of self confidence.
- Give them positive encouragement and praise for what they do. Even if they do not succeed every time at every task set for them, you can still praise them for the effort that they put in or for giving their

best shot. You should avoid the child feeling defeated and dispirited.
- Regularly summarise what has been learnt and encourage the learner to reflect on what they have learnt and to verbalise it, or if appropriate, to write a brief summary of what they have learnt in their exercise book.

2.10 Hearing impairment and visual impairment

It is surprisingly common for children to have difficulties with either their sight or hearing. Common enough that we should certainly have an idea about how to make the school environment and learning in our classrooms accessible for them!

Often, if a child is completely deaf or blind, they may be unable to access a non-specialist school environment, and so they may be allocated a place at a specialist provision that can meet their needs. Children in the *'grey area'* who have some difficulties with vision and hearing will turn up fairly frequently in our career and it is relatively simple to make a few adjustments for them in the classroom.

The causes of visual or hearing impairment can be a very wide variety of things ranging from it being present since birth, the result of some other illness in childhood that caused the condition, an accident they were involved in, or even a degenerative condition. The causes for how an individual came to have a visual or hearing impairment are perhaps less important to know, but it is important that we should know what to do differently to support them.

We will now look at some of the easy adaptations that we can introduce into our classroom in order to make education more accessible to these learners.

Adaptations for the visually impaired

- If you have information on display for the class to follow, provide the learner with their own print out of

this. Be sure and use a font that they are happy with and a sufficient font size that they can read with greater ease.
- It may help some visually impaired learners to have additional lighting. Also ensure that the classroom is well lit so that they may benefit from this.
- They may well benefit from being seated near the front of the class if this works for their eyesight. They may be able to read things on display easier if they are seated near the front. Discuss this with the child.
- Use high contrast colour schemes on your whiteboard, smart board and any print outs.
- Try to give them objects to experience rather than just pictures on the screen. For example, if teaching maths around currency, ensure that they have a physical counterpart to manipulate with their hands.
- Information that is presented in writing, e.g. presentation software, white board etc, must be read aloud so that the learner has a chance to take it in. They could be given a copy to put on their laptop.
- If pictures are used as part of the lesson, describe what the picture is.
- If it is a lesson where students might raise their hand to answer a question, consider getting the learners to clap 2 or 3 times instead of raising their hands. A learner can do this and it gives the visually impaired child a better chance to engage.
- Give clear verbal instructions to the class. For example *'pass your book forward to the person in front of you and also take the book which is being passed to you from behind and pass this forward'*.

- Assistive technology - the child may need access to specific types of software to access their learning. Your school should really already have a policy on what is provided and how. If they do not have this in place, talk to the child and see if there is anything that they use at home that they could be provided within class. They may need access to a school laptop. There should really be funds allocated for this in an ideal world. If not you may have to go to the IT department and see if they have an old laptop that could be refurbished.

Adaptations for the hearing impaired

- Face the learners when you are talking. A child with hearing impairment may use a mixture of their hearing and lip reading. Ensure that your lips are visible when speaking to the class as this may help them understand and engage.
- They may benefit from being seated at the front of the class.
- Try to avoid an overly noisy environment as much as possible. This may help sounds to seem less muddled and sound may be easier for them to process.
- Provide the hearing impaired learner with printed material so far as possible to supplement what is delivered in the class. This may help them to access the lesson.
- Adaptive technologies may be needed by the child and they may need to have a laptop in class to work from. Hopefully the school will have a plan in place to support them. If not, you may have to do some research and experiment with the best way to

support them with assistive technologies. Be sure and ask the child if there is anything they use at home that could be incorporated into lessons.
- Check for understanding and check that the learners have heard you ok. If they have not, repeat and rephrase what you have been saying.
- Pre-teach new vocabulary. If the next lesson will involve new words that the child may not already know, give these to them to take home and study. This may enable them to learn the specific vocabulary of a subject ahead of it being required.

2.11 Anxiety disorders

Anxiety is not something uncommon for humans to experience. It can be a natural response to some kind of pressure or an event that may happen in life. Anxiety can be characterised as an unpleasant feeling of worry or nervousness in response to something around us or to thoughts that we are having.

When anxiety kicks in, the body responds by releasing hormones which might be associated with a *fight/ flight/ freeze* response and the heart rate can become elevated and the breathing more rapid.

Whilst it is normal enough to experience anxiety sometimes, when it happens with great frequency or becomes a semi-permanent state, this is problematic, and it can be part of a broader mental health condition which may require treatment.

In some children (and adults) anxiety can become very problematic when it arises very frequently. It can be additionally problematic when it is disproportionate to any actual threat or even if the threat is imagined and is not present outside of the imagination of the child. When a child's anxiety levels get to this height, it can seriously impact on their well-being and their ability to interact with the world around them in a happy and productive way.

When anxiety reaches a certain point in its severity, it is sometimes diagnosed as an *anxiety disorder*. This tends to be when the anxiety is pervasive, extreme and very regular if not continual.

The most common varieties of *anxiety disorder* are:
- Generalised Anxiety Disorder - when someone persistently experiences heightened levels of anxiety for weeks or months and it impacts their ability to lead a normal life.
- Panic Disorder - when someone experiences panic attacks on a regular basis that are usually unrelated to any real world threat. Having a panic attack does not mean that someone has panic disorder, but if these are frequently happening and are unrelated to what is happening around a person, it may be panic disorder.
- Social Anxiety Disorder - this is when someone experiences intense fear/anxiety of social situations and social interaction. It can become extreme to the extent that someone may feel unable to leave their house. A common aspect of Social Anxiety Disorder is a strong fear of being judged by others. This could be about physical appearance, clothes, ability or any number of things that a person may fear they are being judged about by strangers or those in their environment.
- Selective Mutism - this usually emerges in children before the age of 5 years old. A child who suffers from selective mutism will not usually have difficulties with the development of language and will usually be able to talk under some circumstances. Generally, they will feel anxious in some situations, such as a social situation, and will feel unable to talk and so will appear to be *mute* when this happens. Most children with this diagnosis will also have an anxiety disorder.

Not every child with anxiety will require specialist intervention and it may be something which passes for them. Some children will experience such severe and frequent anxiety that they will need some specialised support or even medication to help them cope.

Supporting Anxiety in school

Some of the following may help you to support a child with an anxiety disorder or one who is experiencing heightened anxiety.
- Be available to talk with the child if they are experiencing heightened anxiety and want to discuss it.
- Do a session with your class on anxiety, how anyone can experience it, what it is and suggest coping strategies that they can use to deal with it if it happens.
- Do not minimise a child's feelings and tell them they are being silly. Communicate with them, listen to them, take on board what they are saying and see what you can do to support them at that moment in time.
- Discuss with the child if there is anything that they know works for them to de-escalate anxious feelings. They may not have any coping strategies, but there may be something that makes them feel less anxious. If there is a way that you can incorporate this into the day or even that they can use this in class, then it is possibly a good idea to do so.
- Design the school day to have a clear and predictable structure. Be very clear on expectations

for what the learners are supposed to be doing. Such an environment may be less likely to induce anxiety
- The child could be encouraged to listen to calming music on headphones if this is workable in class
- You could have a designated *calm space* that the anxious child could retreat to when they are feeling overwhelmed. Depending on the type of school, this could be in one corner of the classroom or it could be somewhere agreed and safe outside of the classroom
- Vigorous physical activities can be healthy for children with anxiety and this is something that could be encouraged. Also, time in nature is healthy for young people with anxiety. If this can be figured into their day then that is positive but this may be difficult to achieve in some schools

OCD (obsessive Compulsive Disorder) is another condition which is related to feelings of anxiety and can sometimes be extreme in how it manifests. OCD is different for different people but often it will
- Involve obsessive thoughts or intrusive thoughts which are difficult to banish from the mind of the sufferer.
- There will be a response to the obsessive or intrusive thoughts which is likely to be anxiety and feelings of distress.
- Repetitive and compulsive behaviours that arise as a result of the obsessive thoughts and anxiety (sometimes called OCD rituals)

The compulsive behaviours that arise from someone who has OCD may seem unusual, but can sometimes be soothing to the person with OCD. This is not always the case as the person may feel compelled by forces beyond their control to do the repetitive behaviours.

I worked with one child who used to call the intrusive thoughts they would get their *'OCD voices'* and the only way they were able to get them to stop was by walking backwards and rhythmically chanting the names of the characters from a children's TV show. Their *'OCD voices'* were quite distressing for them and this aspect of their condition could make focusing in class very difficult for them.

Other children could be quite unkind regarding their OCD behaviours. Regardless of their barriers to learning, they actually achieved quite highly in some of their GCSEs with some very careful planning and making appropriate adaptations that were very specific to their needs.

2.12 PDA (Pathological Demand Avoidance)

Every time you are tempted to do something the exact same way, ask yourself if you are actually seeking a different outcome.

PDA or *Pathological Demand Avoidance*, is a condition that has only been identified relatively recently, the term being first used in the 1980s. In the past there has been some debate as to whether PDA is a real condition or not, but opinion now increasingly leans towards PDA being a genuine condition. Occasionally you may see it called *Extreme Demand Avoidance*, but this is less often used than PDA.

PDA is not currently well understood but it has been proposed that it is a part of the Autistic Spectrum. Certainly, it is often identified in people who are known to be on the Autistic Spectrum, but PDA traits can manifest in children who are not identified as Autistic. Further research in the future will likely lead to a better understanding of PDA, its causes and who is most likely to be affected by it.

PDA can be mistaken for other conditions or it may be that a child is simply excessively oppositional; PDA however, is rooted in something different.

PDA likely arises from a mixture of excessively rigid thinking, as can be observed in Autism, and a heightened sense of anxiety in the child. PDA can manifest in such a manner that any kind of demand, instruction, request or even expectation to behave a certain way can result in quite seriously adverse reactions. I have even observed a

PDA child to go into a state of meltdown when they have been asked to participate in one of their favourite activities.

When a PDA child is asked to do something, they may bite, scratch, punch, spit or similar behaviours, possibly triggered by excessive anxiety that they feel and/ or a lack of clear understanding of social cues and behaviour. Demands that could trigger could potentially be as simple as 'put your shoes on, please', or 'be sure and shower before school'.

I once worked with a young boy who had been diagnosed with PDA. He was quite unable to function in a mainstream school setting (he was attending a specialist SEN school by this time) and some of his behaviours could be quite extreme.

When he arrived at the school gates every morning his anxiety would spike so severely that he would attack his mother and any teaching or support staff who were within reach. He would usually calm down after he had reached his designated space, which we had decorated together with pictures of deep sea animals - his primary area of interest.

After I had gotten to know the young man a bit better, I invited him to share with me, if he wanted to, what made the school gates so difficult for him. I suspected that I might hear of a generalised dislike for school, but I was somewhat surprised to discover something that I had not speculated on previously in relation to his daily difficulties at the gate.

He shared with me that *the route he took through the school was extremely disorientating for him and caused excessive stress and anxiety for him because of the number of bends in the corridor and the angles of the stairs.*

I asked the child if he would like to study some architect's plans for the school (I luckily had these to hand from doing some recent risk assessments) and propose a new route that we might use in the mornings to enter the school. He solemnly agreed to do this and took home the plans for the school that night.

The following morning, ahead of arriving at school, we discussed the new route he wanted to take which was mostly around the outside of the school and a little convoluted rather than the direct approach which we had previously used. I could see no potential risks from the route the child had proposed and it would take a minute longer or less, so we all agreed to give it a try.

Miraculously, by taking this route, the child managed to avoid meltdown at the same point every morning and his mother was bitten considerably less often. This was a surprisingly easy win, if somewhat unorthodox.

The moral of the story here is that PDA seems to be anxiety driven. The anxiety may not be caused by what you think or even by something that you fully understand. Try and explore what is making the child anxious with them through conversation if they will engage, and see what small things you can do to change their day to cause them less distress.

In the story above, we made a small change to the routine of the child which while a little unusual, made quite a large difference to their wellbeing and behaviour. Whilst it may well have taken a minute longer to walk to their classroom, I think most people would agree (if they were thinking clearly) that this is actually a better route to take than the child having anxiety so acute that they attack people around them every morning.

It could be challenging to make the necessary changes for a PDA child in a mainstream school (although it can be done), but if they are in a smaller SEN school it may be possible to adapt things to meet their needs so that they are less likely to behave in an extreme way.

The following are some suggestions that I have found useful in working with PDA children. Some may be easy for you to implement, some may be more difficult. It will depend on your setting.

- Make sure that they have a timetable given to them for the following day at the end of each school day. They can be encouraged to study this and to discuss any parts of the timetable that may cause them anxiety with their parent(s) and if they are willing, why it is causing them anxiety. This can then be handed over to the school staff who work with them and this may be able to be planned for by modifying an activity or having a discussion about the activity to reduce their anxiety.
- Allow the child to decorate their working space with images or symbols of things that are important to them. This can help make their space more friendly and appealing to them. If they are more prepared to

engage and learn, it does not really matter if their immediate environment is decorated with pictures of Squid, Pokémon, my little pony, musicians or Marvel superheroes.

- If your setting is flexible enough, or if there is a small PDA group taught separately or if a PDA child is taught by themselves, their lessons and activities for the day could be on a *'carousel'*. This means that the child is aware that they need to complete all of the activities during their school day but they can pick what order they want to do them in. This gives them a degree of control over their day which can relieve their acute anxiety.
- Observe where the flash points are in the day. Is it a particular activity or place that the child tends to become the most distressed in? Be aware of this and try to understand what is happening for the child. Then make modifications, as you can.
- Keep an eye on the child's stress levels. Know what it looks like when they are starting to get agitated. When this happens, scale down any demands that you are putting on them.
- Remain calm. If the child starts to get into a heightened state, do not raise your voice and become equally distressed. This will have the sole effect of sending the child into further anxiety and potentially extreme behaviours.
- Ensure there is a *safe space* that the child can retreat to and attempt to self calm if they are able to. This could be a designated corner of the classroom that is a chill out spot. I have even known one primary aged child with severe PDA to react well to having a small tent (with the entrance remaining open for safety reasons) which they

could climb into to spend five minutes with their stuffed toy. This had the effect of removing some of the excessive stimulus around them and it gave them a chance to reset and then re-engage. This will not be necessary for most children but if a child's behaviours are extreme, you may be required to think outside of the box to help and support them.
- If possible, sit them by themself so that they do not have to share a desk with another child.
- The language you use is important. Avoid making direct statements that may trigger the child, i.e. a phrase that sounds like a demand. For example saying *'it is time to read. Pick up your book now'*, may result in a difficult time. Making the same demand in softer language may yield better results, for example *'I wonder what's over there in the library corner today. Shall we go and have a look?'* could potentially yield better results.
- Give the child options and choices. These can be oriented towards a particular end goal but can be presented in such a way as to appear less menacing to the child. For example, rather than saying *'pick up your pencil and get writing'*, you could try saying *'what colour of pencil do you think would be best to write in today?'*.
- Distract the child with humour. This may be easier to do for some than others, but a well-timed joke or even the cheesiest of 'dad jokes', can sometimes break a building negative mood. Even if it just results in the child berating your terrible joke, it doesn't really matter if a negative mood is broken by that simple act.

In summary, PDA can be a challenging condition for both child, parent and educator, but with the necessary adjustments made by the adult in the situation, the impact of PDA can be reduced in most cases.

2.13 How SEN is classified and defined

Special Education Needs (SEN) is a term which means that a child is assessed as having a learning difference, difficulty or disability which makes it more difficult for them to learn and progress than their peers in some or all areas.

If a child is classified as having an SEN it does not necessarily reflect on their level of intelligence. Many children with SEN can be very bright and intelligent and can potentially be of above average ability in some or many areas. Treat each one that you come across as an individual without making too many assumptions about them.

SEN is something of a blanket term that is used very broadly and so it is useful to know that it is often broken down into four main classifications. In themselves these classifications are still quite broad and include a wide range of conditions. You are likely to find these four categories referenced on the paperwork of a child as being their primary area of need or their secondary area of need. This can serve as a clue when reading their EHCP and assessing what they may need the most support with.

The four areas of classification are as follows:

- Social Emotional and Mental Health (SEMH)
- Communication and interaction
- Cognition and learning
- Sensory and/or physical needs

Social emotional and mental health (SEMH)

In the past, this was called EBD (emotional and behavioural difficulties) which, as a term, is considered to be a bit out of date. This was for a time replaced with SEBD (Social, emotional and behavioural difficulties). I include these out of date acronyms simply because you may occasionally come across them but not because they are really used much anymore.

The term SEMH is most commonly used now, which is a better summary of this classification of SEN.

Children who are diagnosed as having SEMH can have a wide range of difficulties that can manifest in ways such as:

- Difficulty regulating their emotions.
- Difficulty controlling their own behaviour.
- They may be disruptive.
- They may be depressed.
- They may have difficulty socialising with other children or with adults and may be socially isolated.
- They may suffer from anxiety which can be mild or severe.
- They may self-harm.
- They may have eating disorders.
- They may have substance misuse problems.
- They may have attachment difficulties or have suffered trauma.

These are not the only ways that SEMH can manifest but these are some of the more common ones that can be included under SEMH. Every child is different. They may have one or several of the challenges above; they may be almost unnoticeably mild most of the time or their behaviour may be extreme. Each child is different in how they present. Get to know them and read the paperwork that should accompany them.

Communication and interaction

You may find the acronym SLCN associated with this area of SEN. It means Speech, language and communication needs. It means more or less the same thing.

Children and young people who are considered to be in the category of Communication and Interaction of SEN may have difficulty in one or more of the following areas:

- General difficulties in communicating with others.
- Difficulty in understanding what is being said to them.
- Difficulty in communicating their own thoughts in a way which is easy for people to understand.
- Difficulty understanding the conventions of social interaction such as taking turns, reading body language, understanding tone of voice and facial expressions etc.
- Difficulty in forming friendships.
- Stammer/stutter.
- Frustration.

Some children with some of these difficulties will have been referred to a Speech and Language Therapist (SaLT) for assessment.

A SaLT will usually produce a list of recommendations for how staff should work with the child that they have assessed. All staff working with the child should ideally be aware of these and should apply them properly and consistently. This way the child is more likely to make good progress in their areas of need.

The Speech and language therapist may have discrete sessions with the child in order to help them make progress with their own specific barriers and difficulties or they may just roll out a plan for the staff that work directly with the child.

Children with more severe communication and interaction difficulties may use alternative forms of communication like, for example, Makaton.

Makaton is a combination of symbols on cards or a sheet of paper combined with gestures and speech. There are courses you can go on to learn this or alternatively, you can have a look for resources on the internet and pick up a bit of this method of communication on a budget.

Cognition and learning

Cognition refers to the ability to think and use thinking skills. Difficulties that are around learning can range from the mild to the severe. At the mild end of things, this may not impair the quality of life experienced by a child; at the severe end of things it can mean that a child needs substantial support.

You will also find the term *Specific Learning Difficulties* (SpLD) associated with this category of SEN. These are more specific and localised in their effect on the individual rather than being general and affecting most areas of learning.

SpLDs include:

- Dyslexia
- Dyscalculia
- Dyspraxia

This category of SEN is associated with learning difficulties and learning disabilities which are covered in a previous section of this book.

Sensory and/or physical needs

This area can be fairly specialised work and can require knowledge of things such as sign language, but this training may be provided on the job. It is also possible that you may find an evening course in your local area for learning sign language.

Someone with sensory needs may be affected to a lesser, greater or a profound extent, which can have an effect on their ability to engage in learning that is not very carefully tailored to their needs.

This category includes such as the following:

- Hearing Impairment (HI)
- Visual impairment (VI)
- Multi-sensory impairment (MSI)
- Physical disability (PD)

People can be born with these conditions or they can acquire them at various points in their life through illness or accidents.

2.14 The standard classroom adaptation

Teachers in general should accept the fact that whether they work in the most mainstream of schools or a specialist school:

You are an SEN teacher regardless of your thoughts and feelings on this

If around 1 in 10 learners are somewhere on the Dyslexia spectrum, around 1 in 30 have ADHD, possibly 1 in 100 or more have Autism, pretty much every class you teach, statistically, is going to have a learner with some manner of SEN in it.

As the teacher, it is your job to make some effort to be inclusive. If you make no effort to be inclusive, you are going to provide poorly for some of your learners. They will not do as well as they could and they may even grow frustrated in your classes and behave in a manner which is disruptive and not conducive to the learning of those around them. Of course, equally they may just sit at the back of the class and stagnate.

Luckily it is actually quite easy to make a small effort to be inclusive for your learners and it does not have to cost much financially or tax your time heavily, it just requires a small adaptation to be made to how *you* deliver your lessons. Making your lessons SEN inclusive will have no detrimental effect on your non SEN learners.

If you have a laptop at your disposal, as very many of us do in the 21st century, and a projector or smart board of some kind, get into the habit of doing the following things.

Have a PowerPoint or some other presentation software to hand which you can have displayed on your screen. I use a high contrast colour combination. Not everyone will agree which combination is best and some people will find one easier than another, but the one that I use is a mustard background with black text on top. For those who are into their computers, the hexadecimal code for this colour is about #e1ad01.

The font used must be *Sans Serif*, which means straight letters without decorative flourishes at the places that they terminate.

Serif	San Serif
More difficult for Dyslexics	Easier for Dyslexics

Some of the best fonts to use which are installed on a computer as standard the majority of the time include **Arial** and **Comic Sans**. There are fonts which are similar to these such as Verdana and Tahoma which could alternatively be used.

Even better still have a look on a search engine for a free font called *'Open Dyslexic'*. This has been especially designed to be as easy to read for people with Dyslexia as possible.

Some children may comment that the Open Dyslexic font looks a little unusual, but it is perfectly readable to non-dyslexic learners and may make your lessons a lot easier to access for 1 in 10 learners. That's a really easy win however you look at it.

Keep the page of your presentation open behind you throughout the lesson. If you are detailing tasks that the learners need to do, write very brief bullet points on your presentation as you go along. Keep the instructions minimal, uncluttered and to the point. This will help learners with ADHD, ASC and mild learning difficulties to remember what they are supposed to be doing.

You do not have to do this in advance, even though it may be good to prepare a nice presentation in advance if you have time. You can simply type bullet pointed instructions, *on the fly*, as you go along through the lesson. Learners who need to can refer back to these to remind them what they are supposed to be doing and it can help them not to get too off task, distracted or frustrated about what they are doing. This is another extremely easy win and there is little reason for not doing this.

If you have an ADHD learner in the class who thrives on being given a job to do, you could even get them to type the notes onto the screen for you as a special job that they are allowed to do in class. This would constitute a movement break for them and they may thrive on the additional responsibility.

If you are not blessed with a laptop and a display of some kind, as may be the case in some schools where they do not like to spend money on the classrooms, you may have to simply write the bullet points on the board as you go along and be careful not to jumble your writing or use joined up writing.

There are a myriad of other adaptations that you could make, but the ones which I have listed above should really be your *standard classroom adaptation.* This isn't going to make much extra work for you, if any. The minimal amount of effort that is required to do this may pay dividends in terms of the progress which your learners make and how engaged they are in your lessons.

You should also display and discuss the *learning outcomes* for the lessons at the beginning of the session if possible. This way the children will know what they are trying to achieve and why this session of learning is happening. You could get them to write this in their textbooks or just have it on display in the class somewhere prominent if that works better for you.

Section 3 - A more in depth guide

3.1 Safeguarding

> *"There are some corners of the universe which have bred the most terrible things. Things which act against everything we believe in. They must be fought."*
> Doctor Who, 1967.

Safeguarding is one of the most important topics that you will come across in education.

Whilst it may be considered blasphemous by some to state too loudly that if a child fails their GCSEs they can resit them when they are a little older and more ready to do the work involved, it should not be considered controversial to state that a child does not get a second chance at being safe and well looked after during their childhood. That is strictly a one shot deal.

This is why it is *vitally important* that we do our bit when it comes to safeguarding the children we work with.

In this section there will be some reference to abuse which could be triggering and/ or upsetting for some people.

What is Safeguarding and what is child protection?

Very simply put, safeguarding refers to the measures that we put in place to try and prevent harm from happening to a child, whereas child protection is generally what is put in place after something has happened.

If you are working with children, your employer should have a safeguarding policy in place. You should familiarise yourself with this and do your best to meet your safeguarding duties.

It does happen that sometimes a school will have paid someone to write a robust safeguarding policy that the staff have not paid much attention to or do not follow. Occasionally it has happened that a policy has been written which bears no relation to what happens in the school. These are *very* red flags.

Sometimes staff are allowed to sleep through or not really pay any attention to the statutory safeguarding training, or it may not even be delivered. If you come across this kind of sloppy practice it is definitely red flags galore, and it is the sort of thing that any legitimate ofsted inspector worth their pay should pick up on fairly rapidly and be highly critical of in their report.

If the safeguarding practice of those around you leaves something to be desired, be a beacon of good practice and point in the right direction like a signpost rather than assimilating into a negative culture around you.

What's the worst that could happen from poor safeguarding? Someone's childhood could be ruined because staff are negligent in their safeguarding duties. Children have even died because staff have simply not communicated concerns properly or have not paid attention to what is happening around them.

How to respond to a disclosure

It may happen that a child makes a direct disclosure to you (tells you about something that has happened or is happening to them) or they may say something that sounds *'a bit off'* or suspicious and it may raise an alarm bell with you. Whatever the case, you must never ignore something that a child has told you. It could potentially be the only time they ever make this disclosure to an adult and as such you must properly report it, and properly respond to the situation.

This means that you should report it to your Designated Safeguarding Lead (DSL) right away. If you have other things to do, you should not put off reporting it to the DSL or other manager as time could be crucial in preventing a child from coming to harm. Unless the building is literally on fire you should probably go and speak to the DSL right away.

You should have been told who your DSL is on your first day; this is the person within your organisation that is considered to have some degree of expertise in safeguarding and will probably coordinate the response to safeguarding concerns that are reported to them. There is often more than one DSL in an organisation so that there is still a DSL 'on duty' if the other one is off sick or in meetings.

If a child makes a disclosure it is important that you remember the following points:

- Write down what they have said, **verbatim** if possible. That is, write down what they have

162

actually said rather than paraphrase it or put it into your own words. In the event that something that has been disclosed results in a police investigation and it goes to court, what you have written will be evidence and as such, if the language is not that which would usually be used by the child, this could be used to pull a case apart and subsequently an abuser could go free.

- Do not tell the child that you will be able to keep what they have said 'secret'. You must be transparent that you may have to share what they have said.
- Do not finish another task you are doing before you turn your attention to the child. They may change their mind about making an important disclosure.
- Immediately report what you have been told to your DSL and to the senior leadership team. There should really be a DSL on duty/available in the school you are working in at all times, or at the very least, available via phone.
- Failing this, if no one is available to report to, your local authority will usually have a children's services front desk (they may call it something else) that you can ring for advice. They will usually be able to tell you if there is cause for concern and advise you on what must be done.

I will give you an example that I was involved in many years ago. A young student had asked if they could have a chat in private with a Teaching Assistant who they got along with particularly well. The TA obliged and they had a discussion in a room next door to the classroom that wasn't being used at that time.

The child disclosed to the TA that their parent had been hurting them regularly and showed the TA some marks on their body that were accompanied by some traces of dried blood. The TA offered some reassurance to the child, returned them to their class and then told the class teacher very briefly that something was amiss and they had to go and speak to the DSL.

The TA came to speak to me immediately, as I was the DSL for the school. I spoke to the child to confirm what had been said whilst the TA wrote down the child's account of what had happened verbatim. I determined that this was a potentially serious incident and so asked the TA to sit with the child and play some board games whilst I spoke to the local authority's children's services front desk to get some advice as their powers are considerably more far reaching than a school DSL.

Via a quick phone conversation, the children's services agreed that this was a concerning disclosure and called a rapid meeting between a specialist police person and a specialist social worker to determine the course of action to take from there.

Shortly after, I was told that under no circumstances was the child to be allowed to leave the school to go home. This put me in an awkward position as the child's taxi would be along in a little bit to collect them and take them back to their parent who had been accused of physically abusing them. The child stayed put.

The Social worker and Police person rapidly made their way to the school to speak to the child and determine what the next course of action should be.

The TA and I had to wait back after school with the child. We were very careful not to alarm them and to keep them occupied with activities so as to keep them in good spirits. The police person and Social Worker made their assessment and then determined what the course of action should be from there. At that point, it is over to those professionals to take over and work in the best interests of the child.

The parent of the child was beside themself with anger and tried to downplay what they had been reported to have done; but there was evidence there in the physical marks that were left on the child that were consistent with what had been reported.

I praised the TA for her diligence in reporting this to me straight away rather than sitting on the information and hanging around. I assured them that this was absolutely the right thing to have done and that their actions in alerting me to the issue had potentially saved the child from further harm as the issue was now being investigated by the appropriate people.

The phase of work that happens after what has been described here is called *child protection.* This means the measures that are put in place to keep the child safe *after* something has happened. The measures that are put in place can vary from a care order to a discussion.

Types of abuse

There are different ways of categorising abuse but for the purposes of this chapter I will discuss the following main types that you need to consider:

- Physical abuse
- Emotional abuse
- Sexual abuse
- Neglect

There can be overlap between these categories and a child is not always the victim of just one. It is sometimes said that neglect tends to pervade the other forms of abuse listed here but this may not always be the case. We will now briefly look at the main types of abuse.

Physical abuse

This is where someone deliberately causes physical harm to a child. It can include any number of acts such as slapping, kicking, burning, drowning, starving, suffocating, poisoning and any number of other unpleasant acts. Sometimes a parent or carer will pretend that a child is ill and give them unnecessary medication which can cause them physical harm too.

Some signs that may indicate physical abuse include:

- Unexplained marks, bruises, cuts, burns etc.
- The child being very avoidant when asked to explain physical marks.
- The child flinching when there is sudden movement around them
- The child may like to keep a physical distance from adults
- Very subdued behaviour in the presence of the abuser

The above could be indicators that something is happening which other adults should be alerted to.

Emotional abuse

This can be harder to spot definitively than physical abuse. A parent or carer may deliberately act in a manner that is often very unkind towards a child. This can cause the child's emotional development to be affected or for them to develop mental health problems.

For example, a parent may regularly tell a child that they are stupid, worthless, ugly, evil, or not as good as their siblings. Over a period of time this can cause damage to the child. A parent might criticise a child every time that they open their mouth, causing the child to simply not want to speak or to think that everything they say is worthless.

A parent may deliberately terrify a child by misrepresenting things around them in a sinister way giving the child a skewed and unrealistic view of the world around them or causing them to develop a phobia about some aspect of the world around them.

The above are just a few ways that emotional abuse can occur, but there are many other possible avenues for an emotionally abusive adult to take. This can be harder to spot in a child than physical abuse, but nevertheless, if you have suspicions or if a child discloses something to you, take it seriously and report it.

Some potential signs to be aware of include:

- The child may have very low self-esteem.
- The child may have a distorted self-image.
- The child may repeat or paraphrase things that the abuser has said to them which may seem unusual or uncharacteristic of a child to say about themself.
- The child may seem depressed or withdrawn.
- The child may cry unexpectedly and not be able/willing to explain why.
- The standard of the child's school work may unexpectedly decline.
- They may have difficulty in controlling their emotions.
- They may have difficulty in maintaining friendships.

Sexual abuse

This involves, forcing, coercing or enticing an underage child into sexual activities with an adult. The type of activities that take place are easy to imagine, but can include penetrative sex, masturbation, oral sex or any number of other activities.

Sometimes a child is *groomed,* which usually means that sexual activities will be gently approached and there may be a slow blurring of boundaries, leading to more direct activities.

Sexual abuse does not always involve direct physical contact and could involve watching pornography, or making indecent photographs. Sexual abuse can also take place entirely online and so any child's access to the internet should be carefully monitored.

It is also extremely important to remember, whatever your personal views on the subject, sexual abuse is not solely committed by males and there have been many cases where women have been responsible for or involved in very serious offences. Importantly, if you are keeping a safeguarding minded eye on your workplace, do not discount the possibility that female co-workers could equally be up to no good. Keep an eye on everyone equally. It may be uncomfortable to consider, but *anyone* can potentially be an abuser.

Child on child, also known as peer on peer sexual abuse, is also something to be aware of. If you work in a large school, the likelihood is that this will be happening somewhere. Sometimes a child that has previously been sexually abused can act in a manner that is highly inappropriate towards another child who may or may not be consenting. Sometimes this can be done to younger children by an older child.

Sometimes this may happen because a child has a flaky sense of what is consent or they may simply not understand the concept. This can lead to all kinds of inappropriate behaviour which could cause considerable distress and upset to the target of such unwanted behaviour.

As a matter of priority, I always encourage teaching staff to do age appropriate sessions on consent and put out the right messages to children of all ages on the subject of consent. It is absolutely vital that even very young children understand what consent is.

Equally, I think it is important to do a bare minimum of one session on what a *healthy relationship* actually looks like in practice. Some children will not have actually seen what a healthy relationship looks like and so may struggle to recognise if they are being exploited or groomed. Teach children what this and consent means.

Some signs to look out for

If a child is being sexually abused you may potentially see some of the following changes in their behaviour

- You may find that their general mood suddenly takes a downturn and they seem like a different child or may become depressed and withdrawn. They might seem preoccupied with something.
- They may start using language or sexualised behaviours that you would not expect them to know.
- They might seem generally frightened or may go to lengths to avoid a particular person.
- They may have unexplained bruises.
- They may complain of pain in their private areas.

Neglect

In short, neglect is when a caregiver fails to meet the basic needs of a child. These could be physical, emotional or psychological needs. In practice, this could mean not providing suitable or sufficient food and water; not providing shelter or sufficient blankets in winter time; not looking after a child's emotional state etc. It could be allowing the child to go unsupervised for long periods of time or letting them roam the streets beyond a time which is sensible for them to be out. There are many forms this can take.

A possible measuring stick for neglect, that you could consider, is *Maslow's hierarchy of needs*. This is a scale represented in a pyramid diagram which a psychologist called Maslow developed in the first half of the 20th century. It is still a useful tool.

This shows the needs of an individual on an ascending scale. If the needs on the first tier of the diagram are not met, it is difficult for the person or child to grow and develop healthily.

The more secure each step of the pyramid is in the needs of the individual being met, the more they will grow healthily and develop as a person.

The highest tier of Maslow's hierarchy is *self-actualisation*, which can mean different things for different people, but it basically means to become the best versions of yourself, to strive to become more, to realise your full potential.

If the first four steps on the scale are secure and met, it is more likely that the individual will be able to *self-actualise*. Examples of self-actualisation could include creating art, writing a book, learning to play the harp, being creative and satisfied in being creative, having a feeling or purpose and happiness in life, doing great deeds, realising your dreams and ambitions etc.

In short, if someone is always worried and anxious about where their next meal is coming from, if anyone loves them, if they will be homeless in a weeks time and similar things, they are unlikely to achieve great things and if such pressures characterise their existence, it is entirely possible that they will develop mental health problems which could have a profoundly negative effect on them and even the world immediately around them.

Maslow's Hierarchy

- Self Actualisation
- Esteem needs (recognition/ status)
- Social needs (belonging/ love)
- Safety needs (security/ protection)
- Physiological needs (Food/ Shelter)

Maslow's hierarchy of needs is not without its critics, just to acknowledge that. As a lens through which to consider neglect, specifically the first three tiers of the pyramid, it is a useful tool.

It is sometimes said that neglect can pervade the other three types of abuse listed above and whilst this is not always the case it is certainly true that neglect can certainly accompany the negative behaviours of an abusive caregiver.

There are various signs that a child may be neglected.

- Are they often unwashed?
- Are their clothes dirty, the wrong size for them or in a poor state of repair? Ripped, worn out etc?
- Are they skinny or always hungry?
- Do they steal food from other children or appear to have a high degree of anxiety about food?
- Do they have rotten teeth or never seem to have brushed their teeth?
- Do they seem to have a lack of medical care? Things like glasses not being provided or not being immunised?
- Do they seem to be very small for their age?

Any of the above can be attributed to other things but could also be a result of neglect. If you suspect something is going on, don't keep it to yourself, discuss it with management, DSL and SENCO.

Be vigilant for warning signs

There can be many, many warning signs to look out for and some things which could be interpreted as evidence of abuse could equally be caused by something completely unrelated. We have looked at a few in the previous sections.

Keep a vigilant eye at all times.

Does a child have unexplained marks on them? Have you got suspicions? Report it.

One time I observed what looked suspiciously like cigarette burns down the arms of a teenage child I worked with a long time ago. I was extremely concerned about what might be happening there and I tried to speak to them regarding it.

They were instantly dismissive and refused to enter into conversation with me about it. I reported it to the DSL and further pursued the matter with the child when it was just the two of us in class the following lunch time.

After some back and forth they told me that after school they were involved in contests where they and siblings held lit cigarettes between their arms as they burnt down. Whoever managed to hold the cigarette for the longest, i.e. endure it burning their flesh, was considered the winner and would receive praise and reward for this by their immediate family and relatives.

This was a frankly bizarre form of competitive child abuse done by the immediate family that was visibly injuring the child. The children were so used to this behaviour that they did not really see it as abuse and thought this was common enough behaviour. This was handed over to social services to investigate and deal with.

I tell this anecdote to make you aware that strange things do happen both in and outside of school. Be curious about the lives of the children you interact with and pay attention to what is happening around you.

A child may make a direct disclosure to you about something that is happening or has happened. This is perhaps the easier and more clear cut type of abuse to document and deal with.

A child may seem to be in an emotionally volatile state, have mood swings or suffer from depression. This could possibly be caused by some form of abuse, especially if it is a sudden and unexplained change in behaviour and seems out of character for them. It could also be caused by many other things. Keep an open mind and report anything that you see or suspect may be happening.

Go on the record with it via whatever system your school employs for safeguarding reports. Then if other members of staff spot and document similar things to what you have seen or suspect, you have a pattern that makes the balance possibly more likely that things are happening which should not be.

Grooming

Grooming is a process that occurs, usually but not exclusively, when an adult builds a relationship with a child, usually where the child will trust them, where the groomer will have the express intention of exploiting them in an undesirable way at some point during the process or as an end goal of the grooming process.

The person doing the grooming may ingratiate themselves with the family of a child or they may be unknown to the family. If they are known to the family and are popular with them, it may cast suspicion away from their activities.

I recall a teacher who spent some length of time ingratiating themselves with the family of a child from their classes who they had secretly developed an unhealthy interest in. After some time, they eventually bought a holiday for the whole family to go on (who were not very well off). They were caught abusing the child whilst on the holiday. Very unpleasant stuff.

A groomer will sometimes present themselves in such a way as the child may believe them to be romantically involved in a secret relationship. They may exploit a position of trust to do this, or they may approach the child outside and start talking to them. If a child is neglected, they may give them gifts and pay lots of attention to them which may seem to be a very good thing to the child.

Some possible signs that a child may be the recipient of grooming could be, but are not limited to

- The child having unexplained money or new items which they could not have afforded by themself. They would generally not want to elaborate on where these had come from.
- The child having or talking about having an older boyfriend or girlfriend.
- Being very secretive about where and how they are spending their time. They could have unexplained absences from school.
- Being involved in underage drinking or drug taking. The groomer may supply them with this as part of the grooming process.
- Sometimes a child may express knowledge of sex which seems inappropriate or unusual for their age.
- Sometimes a child may act in a sexualised way which suggests that they have been involved in sex acts which are illegal or inappropriate for their age group.

If you suspect that a child may be being groomed, report it to your management straight away and document any evidence that you have that this may be happening.

If the child is willing to talk to you about it, document what they say as verbatim as possible. Report this to your safeguarding lead straight away and also the senior leadership where you work. It is not out of order to ask them for an update on what is happening so that you know what action is being taken.

Remember, if your school is not doing safeguarding properly and is ignoring a problem that is worrying you, you can seek advice from the children's services of your local authority or speak to the police. Don't be afraid to take action if you do not feel something is being taken seriously.

Vigilance in the workplace

It is a truly uncomfortable thought, but can we say with absolute certainty that all of our co-workers are categorically, completely safe to work around children?

It is unsettling to consider that something untoward may be happening in the place that you are working, possibly even done by people that you may share a coffee with or even consider to be friends, but this is the reality of it - *it happens.*

It is your duty to keep an eye out for anything that seems not quite right and to report it. When you see or hear something suspicious you must make a full report to your DSL or head teacher straight away, regardless of who the report is about.

If the suspicion is about the DSL or head teacher or you suspect collusion between staff members to cover something up, you may have to report outside of your school. You can speak to someone at the children's services front desk of your local authority, speak to the police or contact LADO (Local Authority Designated Officer) in order to discuss your concerns. Any of these people will be able to advise you or may get involved.

Bad stuff can happen in schools despite the best efforts of the HR department to follow safer recruitment guidelines to prevent dodgy people from gaining access to children in schools. Checking their DBS only actually works if they have already been caught and convicted for something and there are some slippery people in the world.

This is a very serious part of your duty. Be vigilant and report what you see and hear. If you notice the children have a strange nickname for a member of staff or regularly describe them as 'a perv' or something of that sort, be sure to pay close attention to what is being said. Of course it is not unheard of for children to make things up sometimes, but even so, you report what you hear to the appropriate people, just in case.

An abuser who has insinuated themselves into a school or other setting where they work with vulnerable young people may well seek to befriend the most senior people that they can. If those people are a bit flaky in their practice this can cause serious problems.

For example, in one school that I am aware of, what turned out to be a very dodgy member of staff was employed by the management without properly obtaining references from their recent employers, which should have been done as part of *safer recruitment*.

This person's first priority, on commencing employment, was to establish a flirtatious relationship with the head of that school, who they were some 30 years younger than; they would compliment them, make suggestive comments and generally suck up to them in a way that several members of staff found quite uncomfortable. Unfortunately the head of this school was receptive to this form of manipulation and became so taken with the dubious member of staff that they would hear no ill spoken of them, regardless of what was said.

Some of the regular staff started to notice that this teacher's interactions with the children were not quite right and the boundaries there seemed to be somewhat blurred. This member of staff was just too 'touchy feely' with the kids and had additionally been reported to have pinched a couple of staff members behinds in the cramped coffee room.

Later they were reported to have discussed sex and smoking cannabis in class with some children as young as KS3 and I am not referring to a PSHE lesson. People began to raise their concerns with the head of school who was also the only DSL for the school. In this instance they were told that it was *professional jealousy* and that the teacher in question was *marvellous* at their job and beyond reproach.

Not too long after the DSL had shut down complaints about them, the highly questionable staff member started to push the idea of leading camping trips where he would take a selection of the children away with him overnight.........

You may be getting a rising sense of dread about this scenario and you would be quite right to do so. Luckily a member of staff decided to bypass the ineffective DSL and took ownership of the situation and involved external agencies before anything too terrible had happened. Thus an extremely serious incident was averted.

Never assume that the people above you are automatically on the ball when it comes to safeguarding and generally if you feel something is off and the 'powers that be' in your school are idle, get an external opinion.

It might not make you popular with your manager (it might even make you hated) but it could prevent something absolutely dreadful from happening to a child and frankly I would choose finding a new job over enabling child abuse to happen by not doing anything; that's not something you want to live with having on your conscience.

Interestingly, it transpired later, that the dodgy member of staff described above had been in trouble at their previous place of employment but had managed to wriggle out of a situation where criminal charges would ideally have been made against them and they had resigned their post.

There had been no referrals made to LADO (as there should have been) and the lack of proper references being sought by their new employers (in keeping with safer recruitment) prevented their new employer from being forewarned about them, even if only verbally rather than in the written reference.

The moral of this is, that if people had been doing their jobs properly in terms of safeguarding, this person would never have been able to get a foot in the door, let alone behave improperly around children.

Your duties around safeguarding should be taken seriously and you should always pay due diligence to what you need to do.

LADO

LADO (Local Authority Designated Officer) refers to the person, or more usually a team of people who work for the local authority. Schools and other educational settings have a duty to report any allegations made against the adults who work with children. LADO will advise if there is further action that needs to be taken, such as informing the police etc, or if that which is being reported does not meet a threshold for further investigation. LADO will also liaise with police and other external agencies as required to swiftly resolve any matters.

LADO should be contacted for the following reasons:

- If an adult member of staff has behaved in a way which has harmed or might harm a child.
- If an adult member of staff has possibly committed a criminal offence against a child.
- If an adult member of staff has behaved towards a child or children in a way that indicates he or she would pose a risk of harm if they work regularly or closely with children.

- If an allegation is made against a member of staff by a child or another member of staff.

It is important to inform LADO of allegations that are made for a number of reasons. One of these, quite importantly, is that LADO can hold records for various individuals detailing complaints or allegations that have been made against them in the past.

Imagine if you will, a member of staff has something maliciously said about them by a particularly angry child which on investigation turns out to not have substance and the child admits that they made it up to get even with that staff member. A fairly horrible thing to happen. You should have no fear of LADO holding a record of this to be honest.

Now imagine if you will that an adult who works with vulnerable children has allegations made against them in various jobs that they do over the course of a decade. The allegations are all remarkably similar in tone and content but this member of staff manages to avoid consequence or there isn't enough proof to bring charges, or maybe even that the management are too busy planning their next golf match.

LADO could be extremely useful in this instance as they would be able to document and see the pattern of likely behaviour for this individual which could contribute to an outcome if this member of staff is under investigation.

When a member of staff is found to have done something seriously wrong, as well as the potential legal consequences, they should be referred to the DBS (Disclosures and Barring Service) who will flag them up on an official basis as someone who is no longer allowed to work with children or vulnerable adults.

If a person who is barred applies for employment with a school or similar and that place is doing the bare minimum in terms of safer recruitment, a DBS will be raised or the DBS will be checked online and their unsuitability for employment will be flagged up hopefully prior to them so much as setting a single foot in a building with children in it.

Some other Safeguarding issues to be aware of

I will now give you a brief description of a few safeguarding issues that it will be useful for you to be aware of. If you suspect that any of these may be happening, document and report appropriately.

County lines

County lines is the generic term for a specific form of criminal exploitation of children. This usually involves a child being persuaded, coerced or forced into one or more of the following:

- Holding illegal drugs for a gang which they intend to sell and sometimes holding money which has been generated from drug dealing.
- Dealing drugs on behalf of the gang and giving the gang the proceeds or the majority of it.
- Transporting drugs for a gang from one location to another. This is often from an urban area to smaller towns or coastal towns.

These activities are delegated to children for the fairly obvious reason of the criminal gangs avoiding prosecution. The gangs that run these types of activities can range from the well organised to the newer and more opportunistic.

The methods of coercion used to force young people into these activities can include threats of violence to them or their families. If caught by the police, the expectation would be that the child would not implicate any of the gang members for fear of reprisals against them or family members, so the child involved in county lines who gets caught may well get a criminal record or other serious consequences.

Some children are enamoured with the gang lifestyle and may think that drug dealing and crime are somehow glamorous and it may be quite easy for a gang to recruit such a child, who may feel that what they might perceive as acceptance to a gang is a rite of passage for them.

A child may even view themselves as an equal partner or business partner with the person they are dealing with. They may regard themself as being 'in' with that group of people. The reality is often quite different and such a gang will usually only be interested in them whilst they have a use for them.

Some gangs will deliberately get a child into debt with them, possibly through loaning them drugs (referred to sometimes as 'ticking'). Sometimes a child will be 'ticked' a large amount of drugs which they will subsequently be mugged for directly afterwards by a friend of the gang. The gang could then exploit the debt that the child owes them to make them transport drugs or to carry out other criminal activities for them to work off the debt.

Code words that you may possibly hear a child use who is involved in county lines can include, but are not restricted to:

- Running a line
- Going crunch
- Going country

These are generic slang phrases and gangs may well have their own code for their own criminal activities. Keep an ear out for anything dodgy sounding which you may not understand and seek advice if you are concerned. If you hear a child using a weird phrase or slang which you are not familiar with, have a look on a search engine for it or ask colleagues if they know what it means.

Occasionally, children may be trafficked to different areas of the country to work for a gang. They would usually not be treated well during this and may stay in accommodation that is part of something called 'cuckooing'. This is where a vulnerable adult with, for example, physical or learning disabilities or mental health issues has their house taken over by a gang in order to be used for their purposes. This could be used to house children who are working for them or to stash away drugs, guns or other illegal materials or to use as a grow house for drugs.

This kind of criminal exploitation of children is a very serious matter and violence often pervades gangs, so a child who has become involved could potentially come to serious harm.

Some warning signs that a child could be involved with county lines include:

- The child seems enamoured with the gang lifestyle or criminality.
- The child may go missing from school and home for long periods of time and may be very unwilling to explain their absence or discuss their whereabouts during this time. If they are found and brought back, it may be from areas that they have no obvious connection to, i.e. they are sent there by a gang to run an errand and they have no known friends or family members there.
- The child may suddenly seem to have more money than usual or may have items such as expensive trainers or jewellery that they might not usually have.
- The child may have unexplained bruises or wounds.
- They may have more than one mobile phone and/or sim cards that are not explained.
- They may receive unexplained text messages and phone calls at unusual hours.
- There may be a sudden change in the slang and language that they use, indicating that they may be hanging around with a different crowd than usual.

There are many possible signs that a child may be involved with county lines and criminal exploitation. If you are worried that a child may be at immediate risk of harm, or if they have made a disclosure to you that they are in danger, it may be best to call the police directly and seek advice from them. You would of course contact your DSL immediately to get guidance.

You can also contact the child protection services that are maintained by your local authority. Their contact details will be available on their website if you do not already have them. There is usually a relatively fast turnaround time on contacting child protection and getting appropriate advice on what to do or how to proceed.

Often, if a child or young person has become involved in the local gangs and gang activities, the safest way for them to exit this definitively is by moving to a different area where they will not encounter members of that gang or be known.

Radicalisation and Prevent

Unfortunately, some people seek to 'radicalise' children. There are a good many beliefs and ideologies that are largely harmless for a child to explore as part of their development of their own individual world view, but there are a few which are firmly linked to violent attacks, terrorism and other antisocial behaviours.

The way that the media reports on terrorism can be quite unbalanced. Often a white person on the far right will be described as a 'lone wolf with mental health problems' or something similar, whereas someone from an ethnic minority may be described in an entirely less sympathetic light. This can lead us to believe that the problem with extremism can lay solely with particular sections of society who can be somewhat demonised.

Traditionally, someone with extremist beliefs, such as a Neo-Nazi, may have sought to recruit young people in person, looking for troubled or disaffected youths to peddle their toxic views to. This is increasingly done online now.

Sometimes, online gaming can be used as a platform to recruit children into far right ideologies, so this should be something that you keep an ear out for. The parent will of course have more influence over this sphere than a teacher and some joint working may be required around an issue like this.

Grooming into toxic ideologies can be quite a well organised activity and children may be approached through social media (Facebook, Twitter (x), Instagram etc) and slowly groomed into racism, blaming the world's problems on minority groups and even terrorist acts and street violence directed against minority groups.
It is important to warn the children you work with about this and hopefully your school will already have some sessions in place to educate them about this threat.

It is important to recognise if a child suddenly starts to exhibit some behaviour which could be consistent with being groomed into an extremist ideology. There could be a change in the way that they relate to the people around them, suddenly being hostile to ethnic minorities or other minority groups such as LGBTQ+.

They may say strange things in praise of fascist dictators from the past or express violent ideas that they believe are solutions to what they perceive as the 'problems in society'.

If you suspect that a child is being radicalised, immediately report this to your DSL and Prevent officer. They will be able to investigate and refer the child for support as required. It is fine to ask your DSL/Prevent officer how this is proceeding and to ask for an update about what is being done.

FGM

Female Genital Mutilation is a cultural practice that is highly illegal in the UK. It is important to note that this barbaric practice is not religious nor is it recommended in any religious books.

For perceived reasons of purity, some adults will take it upon themselves to have their daughter 'cut', which means that areas of the vagina will be removed in often unsafe conditions by someone who is not medically qualified. The amount of tissue that is removed varies but can extend to the labia and clitoris being removed. There is detailed information available about this online to research.

This is done to children who are too young to consent to this procedure and are too young to properly understand what the implications of this kind of procedure are for their future enjoyment of a sex life.

It is done very much in secret because it is highly illegal in the UK. Often, a child will be taken out of the UK for this to be done abroad during an extended holiday. Sometimes it is performed by a family member who specialises in this and they might visit them in the UK specifically to do this.

If you have any suspicions that a child you work with is about to undergo FGM, you are instructed to directly report it to the police immediately and your DSL secondly. This is not the usual arrangement but time could be of the essence if a child may be put on a plane at any moment and subjected to FGM.

Some alternative names for FGM are female circumcision, cutting, sunna, gudniin, halalays, tahur, megrez, khitan. Some warning signs could be that a girl is discussing a trip abroad for a 'special procedure' or 'operation', that may 'prepare her for marriage' or 'make her a woman'. The girl may even potentially plan to run away from home. The family could be planning a long holiday abroad, perhaps over the summer holidays.

It can be very difficult to spot that FGM is going to happen to a student because it is done under such secrecy. If you have suspicions - report them immediately.

Policy and legislation

Your school will have a safeguarding policy which should be available to all (it should be on their website if they have one) and should be part of the introductory training provided to all workers within the school.

The local safeguarding policy will be based on national legislation, issued by the DfE (Department for Education), but to show how this is reflected at a local level, i.e. within the school.

There are various pieces of legislation to be aware of but one of the foremost is **KCSIE** (Keeping Children Safe In Education). This is updated at least once a year (usually

September) and all workers within the school are expected to be familiar with the contents.

At the time of writing, KCSIE contains the following sections:

> Part 1: safeguarding information for all staff.
> Part 2: the management of safeguarding.
> Part 3: safer recruitment.
> Part 4: safeguarding concerns and allegations made about staff.
> Part 5: child-on-child sexual violence and sexual harassment.

The guidance in KCSIE is statutory, meaning that it is not optional and it lays out the expected standard for how a school should do things, for example, *Part 3: Safer recruitment*. Have a read and compare to how you were recruited - this will give you an idea of how on the ball your school is in this area.

Regardless of how strong or weak your school is on safeguarding, some of the key takeaways from this chapter should be as follows:

- Safeguarding is everyone's responsibility. Your responsibility, the cleaning person's, the head teacher's, the DSL's - Everyone. No exceptions.
- Safeguarding should run through everything that a school does.
- Safeguarding should be of primary concern at all times.
- Be vigilant.
- Be curious.

- Report appropriately as soon as you have a concern and listen to what the DSL says (unless they are clearly doing a very poor job, in which case seek other opinions on the issue or outside help).
- Feel free to follow verbal discussion with other members of staff such as the DSL with an email summarising your concerns. This means that if the DSL does not take appropriate action, you can prove that you raised your concern appropriately when you did.
- If you see something dodgy going on, whistle blow loud and clear.

3.2 - Autism - another look

You will often see this written as ASD (Autistic Spectrum Disorder); Some Autistic people have objected to the word 'Disorder' and prefer to describe themselves as having a *condition*, so that is what I usually call it out of respect for the preferences of some of the people who are diagnosed with Autism.

Additionally, it is important to note that there is also some controversy around the use of the phrase *'Asperger's Syndrome'*. The term is taken from the name of Dr Hans Asperger, a Doctor who did some work around defining autism in the 1930s and 1940s.

Whilst Dr Asperger was not formally a member of the Nazi party of Germany, he was heavily involved with the utterly vile Nazi ideas of 'racial purity' and Asperger was proactive in diagnosing children as having disabilities, SEN or as having *Asperger's Syndrome*.

After the children had been formally diagnosed by Dr Asperger and his colleagues, they would then be taken away from their parents and sent off to 'specialist' medical facilities such as 'Spiegelgrund', where these children who were deemed to be less than human or worthless by the Nazis were used for medical experiments or simply euthanised.

The wholesale slaughter of people with disabilities, mental health difficulties and SEN was widespread in Nazi Germany with something like 250,000 being directly 'euthanised' or killed through 'medical experimentation'. An additional 360,000 people were initially sterilised against their will such as schizophrenics and people at special schools. On holocaust memorial day, remember these people.

Very understandably, a good few people with Autistic Spectrum Condition vigorously object to the name of an utter monster like Dr Asperger being associated with them and Autism diagnoses. After all, Dr Asperger willingly and knowingly sent children such as some of those at your school off to be used for painful human experimentation and a lonely death away from their families. We should never forget that disabled people, SEN children and people with Mental Health problems were murdered en masse by the utterly despicable Nazis. This should remind us that the far right must always be opposed, whatever their rhetoric.

Somebody in your school may tut and roll their eyes about the changing terminology we use to describe Autism - please do feel free to set them straight. We occasionally need to change our use of language to be kind and respectful to one group or another; it really is not that big a deal. If some Autistic people prefer one tag to another, it is really quite easy to respect that where possible and be a nicer person.

Whilst people are born with autism, it is formally recognised after the condition is diagnosed by a qualified professional, such as an educational psychologist. A child (or adult) can be put forward for assessment by a qualified professional; if it is thought that there may be merit to the person potentially having Autism they may be put on the waiting list for assessment. Sadly there are long waiting lists for assessments. This is due to healthcare services not being funded properly by a series of different governments. Some may argue this, but it is the reality.

If a child has parents with sufficient spare funds they can pay for an independent assessment more or less immediately and subsequently their child can access the support they need, allowing them potentially to enjoy a better quality of life. It can easily be said that this represents discrimination toward less advantaged children, through no fault of their own.

Early identification of Autism can be a bit of a lottery. If parents and/or school staff are reasonably well informed on the condition and how to spot it, a child who is Autistic may be picked up in their early years and given additional support and be put forward for assessment.

Sometimes a classroom teacher is not adequately trained on how to spot Autism or a SENCO may be overworked or not sufficiently observant, so a child may fly under the radar in primary and also secondary school and never be identified as Autistic during their school years, when the reality is that they need additional support and intervention to flourish and reach their full potential. This can lead to the child becoming an adult whose quality of life is very much affected by their Autism, perhaps struggling with social interaction, anxiety and understanding people, but never really fully knowing why.

It's quite a sad situation that some children won't get the support that they need and I believe that some training around identifying Autistic children should be mandatory for teaching staff. This is not to unduly increase anyone's workload, but a one hour session on an inset day could really have a positive impact on a lot of children's wellbeing.

The traditional view is that the majority of people with ASC are male. This is increasingly proven to be inaccurate by researchers such as Svenny Kopp. Some of her articles are available to read online if you are curious.

There are a variety of factors that have led to the disparity in Autism being *recognised* in female and male children. The statistics of female and male diagnoses of Autism are not necessarily representative of the actual figures of females and males and *who have* Autism, rather, they are simply a side effect of the traditional understanding of the condition, as we will see shortly.

From a range of interviews with adult Autistic women and careful research it is now being recognised that Autistic girls are actually far better at masking (this means to disguise) their differences than their male peers, and may therefore be more difficult to identify, at a glance.

Much of the research that was done in the past on Autism was done with boys, simply because they were more easy to identify as being Autistic than their female peers because they are not as skilled at masking their condition. This has led to the body of research that mainstream thinking around Autism is built upon to be skewed towards male Autism as the prevalent model.

Subsequently, screening and diagnostic tools are skewed towards male Autistic traits and can barely acknowledge female Autistic traits. As a result of this incomplete understanding of gendered manifestations of Autism, when professionals such as teachers encounter Autistic girls in their classes they are simply not identifying them as such and do not have a discussion with SENCO/parent as they may do regarding their more obviously Autistic male counterparts. Autistic girls may often be thought of by their teachers as 'the quiet one', 'the quirky one', 'sweet but shy' etc.

Some have suggested that the above situation is due to institutional sexism and misogyny, and whilst I fully acknowledge the existence of these things, I would suggest that the situation of gender and Autism diagnosis is more down to the current emergence of a greater understanding of Autism in the field of research. Science is not a complete book.

Clara Tornvall wrote a book called 'The Autists: Women on the spectrum', which is an interesting look into the female experience of Autism. If you wish to learn more about this, the book is still in print at the time of writing.

Some adult women with Autism have described *masking* in their childhood at school, which can be useful to be aware of. Equally, please be aware that this is not a universal female Autistic trait. Some women have described silently observing the social interactions of their peers and then mimicking them in order to fit in as much as possible, often to avoid bullying and social isolation. They have sometimes described being passive and following the decisions of their peers, whether good or not, simply in order to fit in.

As the act of masking or mimicking peers in school is honed over the years, some Autistic women can completely fly under the radar of school staff who are trained (if at all) to look for male Autistic traits. This represents a major issue. The associated problems that can come with Autism such as heightened anxiety, difficulty with social interaction, depression etc are still completely present - there is just a mask placed over this in order to fit in. Maintaining this mask can be an immense effort and can cause mental health problems to develop.

Interestingly, there is some suggestion that Autistic girls may often cease to mask when they return to the family home and may have explosive episodes towards family members as a result of the effort and stress of having to maintain their mask at school all day.

So, what is the big deal about early diagnosis of Autism?

Autism is a neurological and developmental condition. This means that you are born with it and it doesn't go anywhere.

The difficulties that Autistic people can experience throughout their childhood can be present throughout their lives unless they receive appropriate support. The difficulties that can be faced by Autistic people do not magically disappear when they leave school and can seriously affect their quality of life.

Some issues faced by Autistic people can typically be Anxiety, difficulty with social interaction, misunderstanding social interaction or social cues, difficulty with reading the emotions of others and difficulty with expressing their own emotions.

These experiences of life can in turn lead to social isolation, difficulty in maintaining friendships, frustration, depression and sometimes even suicide. To be quite specific, research shows that suicidal ideation, attempted suicide and suicide rates in the Autistic community are disproportionately high compared to the neurotypical population.

What is the solution to this problem? Early identification of Autistic children, both female and male and appropriate interventions being applied by the adults and professionals around them.

There is an abundance of structured interventions for things such as social interaction, communication, regulation of emotions and a host of other structured interventions that are specifically designed to help children (including Autistic children) learn the skills that they will need in order to navigate the world both as a child and as an adult. In my opinion, the earlier a child receives the appropriate support, the higher the likelihood of them not only being a happier child but also being a happier adult.

So, take an interest, get to know your kids, be curious, learn about the indicators that a child may be Autistic and if you think a child may be Autistic, do not sit on your opinion, raise it.

The quality of support for Autistic children in schools can vary wildly from the non-existent to the outstandingly well organised. Hopefully you are working in one of the schools that has a really robust plan in place to support Autistic kids. In which case follow the lead of your benevolent in-house experts and see the magic happen!

If you are not so fortunate and you are working in a school where the SEN provision is not so well organised or may be somewhat absent, do some research (try some of the suggestions in this book) and see if there are some resources that you can find online that you may be able to use with the child to try and help them with specific problems that they may be demonstrating in the classroom or in their interactions with their peers. If you find some good resources, share them with your co-workers.

If a child does not have a formal diagnosis of Autism and they are not getting any support, if they are struggling with Autistic type problems you can see what you can do yourself. Read some literature, have a look at what easy interventions there are that you or a TA may be able to deliver in class. Don't do anything too radical but **do** look into what support you can put in place yourself.

Many years ago, a single mother I knew had a major worry as her daughter had started self-harming and she was understandably concerned. There was difficulty accessing formal support and she could not afford the support privately.

In this instance, I suggested to her, rather than waiting an unknown period to access support, whilst the situation potentially gets worse, we could see what we can do ourselves to support her daughter. We managed to find some resources and CBT based exercises and mindfulness activities that we did with the child, nothing too complex or ambitious, and the situation certainly did not deteriorate.

You may find yourself in a situation sometimes where the support for a child is not present or is not arriving very rapidly. In these instances do some research and see what you can **safely** do yourself in class to support them. I categorically will state though, do not go against the wishes of parents or healthcare professionals in this. No one needs that kind of maverick on the team.

A dangerous myth about Autism

There are a few myths about Autism. Some of these myths relate to stereotyping about Autistic people but some are actually more dangerous. It would be remiss of me not to mention and explore at least one that many people find irksome.

I would like to address the complete myth that Autism is caused by vaccines. I cannot state strongly enough that this should be filed along with other bizarre conspiracy theories that a) have no evidence to support them and b) are not rooted in anything relating to reality.

There is no proper scientific evidence that autism is caused by vaccines. There is certainly no credible research done to a proper scientific standard. Science goes through a process called peer review, which in short means that if someone claims to be a scientist and is drawing weird conclusions from their research or is talking complete hokum, the scientific community calls them out on their lack of evidence to support their claims.

In the internet age, it is very easy for *any* individual to publicise their views, however skewed or removed from reality they may be. This is one of the downsides of the information age. Andrew Wakefield is an individual who has publicised what many consider to be unscientific and unhelpful views.

In 1998 he published a paper stating a link between Autism and vaccines. This was extensively debunked by the scientific community as being poorly researched, unscientific, illogical and having no substance. Wakefield withdrew his paper but his claims continued to circulate as though they were established scientific fact.

His debunked and unscientific 'research' is treated as one of the cornerstones of the 'vaccination causes autism' movement, by those who continue to believe in such things and often loudly proclaim it as a fact to anyone who will listen.

In 2002 Wakefield published another paper making similar claims about a link between autism and vaccines. Wakefield's paper and his ideas were publicly called 'critically flawed' by the wider scientific community due to unscientific methods and irrational conclusions which ignored many of the facts. Still, Wakefield's flawed research is treated by some as the 'scientific proof' of such a link between Autism and vaccines.

There are quite a wide range of scientific papers that have been published that strongly indicate that there is no link between Autism and vaccination. These have survived extensive scientific scrutiny and have been done to the proper scientific standards.

Interestingly, the British Medical Journal published an article in 2012 detailing leaked information about Andrew

Wakefield's alleged plans to use his disproven ideas as a money spinner for his own personal gain. I cannot comment on this but the BMJ have been happy to go on the record with this and the article has been on their website for more than 10 years without being taken down.

So, if previously, you may have seen a meme on social media regarding the link between Autism and vaccinations, please feel free to tell the people posting it that it is based on completely discredited research that has no place in a reality oriented worldview.

Identifying Autism

Formal diagnosis of Autism is a job for a trained professional, but spotting what *might* be Autism amongst the children we work with is very much part of our job. When you think that a child you work with may be Autistic, start a discussion with the appropriate colleagues as soon as you can and be structured in the way that you discuss what you have observed.

In the UK the current diagnostic criteria mostly used by professionals is found in something called the ICD-10. The diagnostic criteria used in America is found in the DSM-V, which you will find mentioned in literature commonly as well, in fact, possibly more commonly than the ICD-10, even in the UK. Feel free to have a look at those publications if you wish but they are written for health professionals rather than the casually curious!

If you are going to go to your SENCO with your suggestion that a child should be looked at for Autism, consider jotting down some notes in a word document or similar and some specific examples of what you are seeing and perhaps the regularity of those behaviours.

Better still keep a diary of what's happening - this would not take the form of prose such as *'Dear diary, today Billy was a pretty cool kid and had cake'*. These would not be useful observations and keeping a record of a child that takes some form like that is completely pointless. It would be far more useful if you detail the number of incidents that correspond to the criteria we will see shortly, with a very brief description of what has been happening and for how long. For example:

'Billy went into a state of meltdown at 12:00 today before he had to leave class for the playground. He remained in meltdown for around 30 minutes in which time he bit the TA. In the afternoon Billy expressed heightened anxiety around making a cake in cookery class. This persisted for about 15 minutes before Billy made a cake'.

If you simply roll up to the SENCO and say *'Billy is Autistic'* you may not actually get that far with it. These things get started on evidence like diaries and observations made by the people who work with the kid.

The following are considered to be definite indicators of Autism that are relatively easy for lay people to observe. Remember, not every Autistic person has to tick every single one of these boxes, they are not all the same and some Autistic girls can mask their difficulties! For a child to likely be Autistic, they would need to display these types of symptoms *regularly* rather than just on one or two occasions.

Anxiety

We may see here, persistent and excessive worry about day to day activities that can cause moderate to extreme distress in the individual.

The worry will generally be disproportionate to what is actually happening and will be disproportionate to the potential risks surrounding the individual or activity. They may become agitated, nervous, tearful, restless, unresponsive or even aggressive.

Possible triggers for this could be but are not limited to - changes in routine, sometimes transitions in activities, ill defined work activities in the classroom, unexpected stimulus like loud noises, social activities or interacting with peers or unknown peers.

Anxiety could also be triggered by specific activities, rules or social conventions that are not understood by the child.

High amount of focus on specific interests or hobbies

It is fairly common for Autistic children (and adults) to have very specific interests which they can become extremely focused on; these can and often do change over the course of their lives. These can range from the relatively mainstream, like the kid I knew who could recite the first 150 Pokémon in the correct order, to the more esoteric such as the child whose area of interest was cataloguing the varieties of wheelie bins in the streets of their local area.

It can be quite astonishing how deep the knowledge of an Autistic child can be in their special interests, like the primary child I worked with who could answer every single obscure question I could throw at them about the biology of the giant squid. Very impressive stuff!

Whilst this can be a real strength for some Autistic children, it can also cause them to neglect their wider learning and sometimes to become hyper focused on their one area of interest to the exclusion of everything else.

Hyper focus on a single area of interest can sometimes make it difficult for them to interact with their peers unless those peers share in their interest to some extent.

Meltdowns and shutdowns

These occur when everything becomes too much for the Autistic child, the stimulus or situation that they are in simply becomes more than they can bear.

Have you ever been in a situation where something made you feel like your head was going to explode? Or have you struggled to regulate the emotions you experienced at that moment in time? Perhaps a dangerous motorist or an extremely annoying person you could not evade? That may give you some insight into how the Autistic child feels at these moments when they go into meltdown or shutdown, caused by events that may seem to be just everyday events to you, the adult.

During meltdown, the child may shout, flip a table, throw themself to the floor, bite, spit, kick, slap, punch or shout obscenities. They may hyperventilate and have difficulty in calming down by themself. This may appear to be very similar to a 'temper tantrum' but it is in fact quite different as it is caused by feelings of being completely overwhelmed and overloaded, rather than feelings of anger.

During shutdown, a child may feel equally overwhelmed by the same or different stimuli or situation but reacts in a different way. At this point they simply feel they cannot cope anymore and they become unresponsive, may stare into space, not speak or may adopt a foetal position or locked position and not respond to attempts to communicate. Both are signs that the Autistic child is having difficulty coping.

Repetitive and restrictive behaviour

Autistic children (and autistic adults) tend to like predictability and routine to a greater or lesser extent. This can present in ways such as having the same breakfast every day, having to do things in a certain order, having extremely rigid ideas about how a given task must be accomplished, what order the pens and pencils must be lined up in, what chair they will sit on and so forth.

Disruption of established routines or self-imposed limitations on activities, can cause the Autistic person to feel intense anxiety or even to go into meltdown or shutdown.

Sensory Sensitivities

Some Autistic people may be overly (or under) Sensitive to specific types of stimulus. These could include

- Sounds
- Smells
- Light
- Pain
- Certain types of fabric

Some Autistic people may for example find that sudden unexpected noises may cause them extreme anxiety (like the school bell that goes off over the course of the day, which some Autistic children live in dread of) or they may, for example, find that it is impossible to filter out the background noises in a classroom and it causes them extreme stress. They may find the sensations from certain fabrics cause them near pain. They may find that physical contact makes them feel extremely uncomfortable.

This can make everyday situations very problematic for them and they may go to lengths to avoid situations where the stimulus which causes them a great deal of difficulty is present.

Social communication

An Autistic child (or adult) can struggle to a greater or lesser extent with social communication and this (along with Social interaction) can be difficult areas for them to cope with. Some signs to look out for around this, include but are not limited to

- Difficulty in understanding tone of voice.
- Not understanding sarcasm and taking it literally.
- Difficulties around interpreting or misinterpreting that which is said to them.
- Difficulties around interpreting or misinterpreting the nonverbal communication, body language or facial expressions of others.
- Needing extra time to process information that is spoken to them.
- Repeating what others say back to them (echolalia).

The above can make it difficult for the Autistic child to interact with their peers and to understand that which is unspoken in human interactions. This can lead them to misinterpret that which is communicated to them in various ways, to take offence when none was intended or to generally misinterpret communication directed to them or around them.

Social interaction

Struggles around social interaction with adults and especially their peers can be a key indicator of an Autistic child. This may manifest in social awkwardness and anxiety in social situations. They may even become avoidant of social situations in general.

The Autistic child may struggle to make and maintain friendships. They may find that social situations cause them considerable anxiety and so they may prefer to engage in an activity relating to their special interest, or some solitary activity and may avoid social interaction where possible as it may seem unpredictable and hard to understand to them.

They may struggle to understand or may not be able to detect how other people are feeling to a greater or lesser extent. They may also struggle to understand what other people's motivations or intentions are. This can make Autistic people particularly vulnerable to a variety of types of exploitation. Equally they may be overly suspicious or negative about other people's motivations. This can sometimes make them appear to be very insensitive (even where no harm is intended).

The lack of comprehension of the conventions of social interaction can sometimes make Autistic children seem to behave in socially inappropriate manners when they do not necessarily mean any harm.

As well as these indicators that a child may be Autistic there are a few other indicators. One that can be present in the classroom is *irritability*. This can manifest at seemingly minor things (or that may appear minor to you) and could potentially be a result of general frustration arising from the other symptoms that can build up, such as those that have been listed over the last few pages. Irritability can potentially be a warning sign that can progress to other behaviours such as aggression or meltdown.

I recall one young person being asked to look for some examples of Abstract Art online. Unfortunately, someone had tagged a photograph of a horse with amongst various other unrelated terms, the phrase '*Abstract Art*'.

The teacher explained to the child that a photograph of a horse did not qualify as Abstract Art, even if it was a very nice horse and that sometimes people on the internet can tag an image with misleading words. The child became highly irritable at this and refused to accept that their horse photograph was not abstract art.

The teacher valiantly tried to move the lesson on (for the sake of the other learners too), but the child would exclaim every minute or so that the horse was Abstract Art, with increasing anger and increasingly wild expletives.

Shortly after, the child went into meltdown and attacked the teacher, also managing to hit a couple of learners in their rage and had to be removed from the class whilst they calmed down. Unfortunately, the child took a good chunk of the day to achieve a state of equilibrium again.

Irritability, potentially leading to aggression is thought to affect around 20% of Autistic children.

The Autistic spectrum

There is currently some difference in how the severity of Autism is described, which can potentially lead to some confusion when discussing the topic with people or professionals. It is quite possible that you will find a mixture of two different ways of categorising the severity and type of Autism used and a variety of different words that are attached to those models. I will briefly (without diving too deeply) look at both so you will have an understanding of these.

One easy way of viewing Autism is as a spectrum. From 'lower functioning Autism' to 'higher functioning Autism' (and various points in between). You will likely hear these terms quite a bit, although they are not usually considered medical diagnoses.

It is a reasonably useful way to conceptualise things, at least superficially. You could broadly generalise that people who are higher functioning are usually more able to navigate the world and use language. People who are described as being lower functioning Autistic may have limited or no use of language and may not be able to live independently. In schools, lower functioning Autistic people may potentially have personal care needs, they may rarely initiate social interaction, and may experience a range of difficulties in day to day life.

Children with lower functioning Autism often go to specialist schools fairly early as their difficulties are often quite easy to identify at an early age. So in practice, if you work in a mainstream school, a PRU, an SEMH school or similar, you are less likely to meet this kind of young person, although it can happen.

Usually, any school that caters for children with severe impairments, like children at this end of the Autistic spectrum, will have comprehensive care plans in place for the children and if you are working in such a school, you would need to follow the plans in place very closely.

In the past Autism was sometimes divided into 5 categories. This model for classifying Autism is increasingly considered to be out of date, but you may

hear *'the five types of Autism'* or a similar phrase used. These were:
- Asperger's syndrome
- Rett syndrome
- Childhood disintegrative disorder
- Kanner's syndrome or classic Autistic disorder
- Pervasive developmental disorder - not otherwise specified (PDD-NOS)

Rett syndrome is no longer considered to be a part of the Autistic spectrum and is recognised as a rare genetic disorder that causes severe physical and mental difficulties, this almost exclusively affects females. It is now understood not to be related to Autism.

More recently a new model was put forward in the DSM-V. This consists of ASD (Autistic Spectrum Disorder) in three levels of severity.

- ASD Level 1 (requires support)
- ASD Level 2 (requires substantial support)
- ASD Level 3 (requires very substantial support)

The eagle eyed amongst you may spot that ASD level 1 corresponds to 'higher functioning Autism' and ASD level 3 corresponds to 'lower functioning Autism', with a convenient middle ground in level 2.

I personally prefer this method of categorising Autism as it seems to me to be fairly straightforward and easy to understand.

Like many types of SEN, our understanding of Autism is emerging and is not yet a complete science.

There was an interesting study published in early 2023 where AI was used to analyse and investigate neuroimaging data (that's brain scans) from a large set of Autistic people and also Neurotypical people. This identified four distinct subgroups of Autism that were previously not known to be distinct. These four subgroups had different levels of activity in some parts of their brains.

Two of these groups had above average verbal intelligence. One had severe deficits in social interaction, but less repetitive behaviour. The fourth had less social impairment and more repetitive behaviours.

It is extremely interesting that such distinct subtypes of Autism are beginning to be identified in the 21st century. This may, in the future, allow for very specific and targeted interventions and therapies to be given to children and adults with very distinct types of Autism as further understanding emerges in this interesting field. This research was done by Amanda Buch and team.

Common classroom adaptations

The following suggestions are fairly easy to implement and will not break the school budget either. None of these are magic fixes, but they could potentially reduce the levels of anxiety and distress that some children experience as a part of their day.

Ear defenders

These are exactly what they say on the tin. If a child has sensory sensitivities in the direction of being startled by loud noise or finds background noise overwhelming, a pair of ear defenders can be purchased quite cheaply for them.

These can either be kept by the child and used as required if they are able to manage this by themself, or alternatively can be given to them by an assistant or the teacher at points when they do not have to listen to the teacher or there is likely to be distracting noise.

It is for the teacher managing the classroom and the children to figure out how best to deploy these. The child having the ability to isolate themselves from the unwanted sounds that may be causing them distress may have a dramatic impact on their mood and ability to focus, and all for a very small fraction of budget.

Weighted blanket

Weighted blankets are a special kind of blanket that has a denser or heavier filling than usual, as it says in the name, so that it weighs far more than a usual blanket.

For Autistic children who particularly suffer from anxiety, the sensation of gentle pressure that this exerts on them can help relieve their anxiety. It is possible that the gentle pressure helps their body to release oxytocin, which can help the child to feel less stressed.

This is another relatively inexpensive thing which may make a difference to the child in their ability to manage their own anxiety or to lower their levels of anxiety.

3.3 ADHD - Another look

I recall, one time a few years back, having to sit through a two day training session on GDPR. Now, as fascinating a subject as GDPR may (or may not) be, I have to confess I struggled significantly with this kind of forced overload of GDPR.

As the minutes of GDPR legislation droning turned into hours, I began to feel a kind of desperation to be somewhere else, the words of the trainer turning into a jumble of nonsense to my ears. I began to fidget in my seat and doodle and generally not take much in.

The trainer, in their defence, tried valiantly to give some life to the subject, but each time they stated *'and I think you are going to find the next bit interesting'*, internally I would retort, *'I very much doubt that mate.'*

By the afternoon of the second day I was beginning to feel numbed and shell shocked, the restless part of my psyche eyed the fire alarm as a possible way to escape the training session, but the part of my mind which deals with impulse control banished the suggestion instantly as the worst possible course of action for my continued employment.

When finally I emerged from the large, seemingly airless chamber of GDPR and felt fresh air in my lungs and sunshine on my skin, there was an incredible sense of relief. I strongly suspect that the majority of other people in that training session felt similarly to me.

Well, I made it through the two day long GDPR training session, with only moderate damage to my wellbeing. I share this tale of adversity and endurance as it is relevant to our understanding of the daily experiences of some ADHD children. They may struggle to remain focused for 5 minutes and may well share how I felt at the GDPR session I have described above after relatively short periods of time. Consider this when you are trying to understand an ADHD child's frustration or lack of focus.

ADHD is a widely recognised developmental condition that can affect a child's behaviour and engagement. If a person has ADHD, it is not a condition that tends to go away with time, but the person with ADHD may learn to manage their condition more effectively as they get older or the symptoms may present in a different way.

Current research presents us with the following statistics around ADHD

- Around 3.6% of boys aged 5 - 15 are considered to have ADHD
- Around 0.8% of girls aged 5 - 15 are considered to have ADHD
- We do not yet know why ADHD (or ADHD diagnosis) is more common in male children.

I have heard some people previously state that ADHD is caused by bad parenting. This is definitely not true. Whilst good quality, ADHD aware parenting can help a child manage their condition better, the opposite kind of parenting will not cause ADHD by itself.

Some of us may recall learning about *'nature vs nurture'* if we, for example, did A level psychology. ADHD comes under nature as someone is usually either born with ADHD or they are not. Nurture can exacerbate the symptoms of ADHD or proper interventions and support can help to minimise its impact upon the life of the person diagnosed with ADHD.

One exception to this is that some people may develop ADHD like symptoms/behaviour following a traumatic brain injury (TBI). How this works is not yet fully understood and there is some debate whether it is ADHD or just an ADHD like presentation.

Some other conditions can manifest in such a way as to appear to be ADHD but are in fact not ADHD. Sometimes attachment disorder can manifest in a way that can be mistaken for ADHD, but this does not in fact have the same cause and so medications intended for ADHD would very likely be ineffective. It is generally going to be the job of a decent psychologist to work out the difference between one condition and another. We will look at attachment disorder in another chapter.

Some research suggests that as high as a quarter of the UK prison population may have ADHD. Research also suggests that many of these prisoners have not been previously diagnosed as having ADHD and so have not received any kind of structured interventions in their lives, to help them cope with their condition.

It is very important to point out that ADHD does not make people automatically criminals or to default to antisocial behaviour. This would be a very unfair generalisation and would suggest a lack of understanding of the situation.

If a person diagnosed with ADHD receives appropriate support in the form of either medication or psychological management techniques, we see a large improvement in their ability to cope. Appropriate management of the condition has been shown to reduce criminal behaviour in men by 32% and to reduce criminal behaviour in women by 40%. Additionally, it is estimated that 80% of the prison population who do have ADHD are undiagnosed.

Putting these pieces of the jigsaw together, I assert without any reservation -

> *As a society, we are failing our children by not sufficiently investing in diagnosis and early intervention*

If we can contribute towards early identification of ADHD in children and contribute towards their receiving appropriate support, we are positively contributing to the quality of their future and also helping society in general.

That various elected governments have consistently underinvested in healthcare for decades is *criminal* in my opinion. That sufficient funds are not allocated for children to be assessed and supported in a timely fashion is *neglect* committed by the state.

We have probably all heard rhetoric from politicians about *'getting tough on crime'*; I personally prefer an approach of getting tough on the causes through early identification and appropriate therapy to support children with ADHD so that they can lead as happy a life as possible.

Young people with ADHD who have not been diagnosed as such and have not received appropriate support, may turn to drugs in order to 'self-medicate' for their condition, which can cause a host of problems in their lives.

Educational outcomes for people with ADHD tend to be worse than their neurotypical peers. This is not linked in any way to their intelligence, but is likely in my opinion to be linked to a lack of adaptation in education to meet their needs and a lack of appropriate support being given.

The long term trajectories of people with ADHD suggest that they are more likely than their peers to become unemployed or to be 'sacked' from work and can do less well in the workplace in general.

I cannot labour the importance of early identification and support enough as it really can be a life saver for a child who has ADHD. Late identification is of course better than it never happening at all, so maintain an attitude of curiosity about the neurodivergence and mental health of the young people that you work with. Have a discussion with the SENCO if you think a child might have ADHD and go on the record with your thoughts.

What causes ADHD?

It is a very sensible question to ask when trying to understand a condition. The simple answer at the time of writing is that *we do not yet fully understand what causes ADHD.*

There are some factors which we are fairly sure are related. Children who are born prematurely, before the 37th week of pregnancy are statistically more likely to have ADHD. Children who are born underweight are more likely to have ADHD. We are not sure how this factors into ADHD yet.

A link has been observed between ADHD and smoking, drinking, opioid use and drug use during pregnancy. This does not necessarily mean that all parents of ADHD children were doing any of this though, so please reserve judgement.

ADHD can run in a family. This suggests that there is likely a genetic cause for ADHD, but this is not fully understood yet. If someone is diagnosed as having ADHD, it is likely that a parent or siblings may have ADHD too. The way that ADHD is inherited (or not) by a child, is not yet understood and is likely to be complex. Future research will likely shed light onto this.

Some research has included doing scans to explore the possibility of potential differences in brain structure of ADHD people and 'neurotypical' people. Scans have been done on the brains of people who are diagnosed as having ADHD and some physical differences have been identified with some variation in size of different regions of their brain, with some regions being larger or smaller than average.

It has been proposed by some that certain neurotransmitters function differently in the brains of a person with ADHD or that there is a difference in the levels of those neurotransmitters compared to 'neurotypical' people that gives rise to some of the behaviours associated with ADHD.

How this all fits together is not yet understood but research is actively being conducted by the scientific community and new breakthroughs in our understanding of ADHD could happen at any time.

Some people have suggested that ADHD is caused by childhood vaccinations. There is literally zero credible research that supports this view and it should be viewed with the same scepticism as reports of tap dancing unicorns.

Some researchers have suggested that rather than being purely a developmental condition, ADHD may actually have been driven by evolution in the distant past of our species. ADHD could have been an evolutionary adaptation to the possibly nomadic lifestyles of our ancient ancestors. What we think of as the associated 'problems' of a neurodivergent person may actually have made them more successful at survival in our past when people probably led hunter gatherer lifestyles in a social group of some kind.

ADHD traits such as vigilance, novelty seeking and the urge for exploration, could have actually been key in the success of some of our ancestors in facing the challenges of securing food, resources and shelter and evading threats before the transition to agriculture and a presumably more sedentary lifestyle in farming communities.

I find this interesting food for thought. If we allow ourselves to consider that ADHD may be the genetic inheritance from our rugged ancestors who passed down the baton of survival through the ice age and other challenging epochs of prehistory, we could conclude that in different times, this difference could have been one of the factors that helped our species to survive, 'neurotypical' and ADHD alike.

Given this, it may become easier to empathise with why ADHD children may struggle to sit still in a chair for hours and hours on end doing sometimes repetitive tasks that may seem meaningless to them. We may need to seek ways that we can channel their differences in a constructive and useful way - ADHD can potentially be a strength for some people.

You may be getting the feeling that there are a great deal of question marks over the exact causes of ADHD, and if so, you would be right. Future research will likely shine a light onto the details of this condition and how it works on a neurological level and how inheritance of the condition works.

However many gaps there may be in our collective understanding of the roots of the condition, we are quite certain about how it presents in everyday life and we also have some interventions in our SEN toolbox that are likely to help the individual with ADHD.

Defining ADHD

When a psychologist is assessing someone for ADHD, they will usually use something called the DSM (Diagnostic and Statistical Manual of Mental Disorders) or its UK equivalent, the ICD-10. This manual contains clinical definitions for 'mental disorders', including many SENs such as ADHD.

These manuals are periodically updated as existing definitions for conditions are changed or the understanding of a condition improves, which can lead us to change our thinking about what defines that condition. You may be interested to have a look at the DSM or ICD-10 which is accessible online but you may not always find it light reading.

I have summarised what are usually considered to be the defining points of ADHD below. Someone does not have to display every single behaviour listed below to be likely to have ADHD, but they do need to meet a given number of the criteria listed.

ADHD is usually considered to have three main components. These symptoms will generally be consistent in their presentation rather than occasional.

- Difficulty in paying attention, being easily distracted - **Inattention**.
- Overactive behaviour - **Hyperactivity**.
- Poor impulse control - **Impulsive behaviour**.

Inattention may be detected via the following symptoms or behaviours:

- They may struggle to give due attention to detail or may appear to make careless mistakes in their schoolwork or other activities.

- They may have difficulty in holding their attention on tasks or play activities.
- They may not seem to pay attention when spoken to directly.
- They may not follow instructions and may struggle to complete or do school work, chores or duties in the workplace - they may lose focus or get side tracked.
- They may have difficulty organising themself in tasks and activities (which may make it difficult for them to complete tasks or activities).
- They may be avoidant or reluctant to do activities that require mental focus and concentration over longer periods of time, like schoolwork.
- They may regularly lose items required to complete tasks or activities, e.g. pencils, pens, calculator, keys, wallet, glasses etc.
- They may be easily distracted.
- They may be forgetful in everyday activities.

Hyperactivity may be detected via the following symptoms or behaviours:

- The child (or adult) may fidget with their hands or feet or tap with hands or feet on a regular basis.
- They may have difficulty in remaining in their seat and may wander at inappropriate times when they are expected to remain in their seat.
- They may run about or climb in situations where this is not appropriate.
- They may be unable to (or find it challenging to) take part in play activities/ leisure activities quietly.
- They may often appear to be 'on the go'; think *relentless activity*.

- They may talk excessively.

Impulsive behaviour may be detected via the following symptoms or behaviours:

- They may shout out an answer before a question has been completed.
- They may have some difficulty in waiting for their turn in activities.
- They may interrupt or intrude on others, for example interrupting in conversations or the play activities of others.

Impulsive behaviours can arguably be the most problematic area of ADHD for the individual who presents with poor impulse control. This can be defined as *acting without giving due consideration to the outcome or consequence of an action.*

For someone with ADHD who has not received appropriate support to help them regulate this aspect of their condition, impulse control can cause serious problems in both childhood and adult life.

For example, it is not unheard of for an adult with this aspect of ADHD to spend money that they do not have and then not have funds to pay for their food shop.

Ever had someone annoy you in the supermarket but you managed to take a deep breath and step back from the situation? A person with poor impulse control may have already thrown something at the annoying person before they have weighed up the potential consequences.

A child with this aspect of ADHD may often do things that seem antisocial or just silly in class. If asked why they were behaving in that particular way, they may not have an answer for you or even understand their own behaviours and where they come from.

Some children with this presentation of ADHD can feel intense shame about their own behaviours but also feel unable to do much about regulating those problematic behaviours. They may feel sadness and a sense of isolation arising from their differences. With appropriate support they may be able to learn to self-regulate better.

Types of ADHD

A person with ADHD will not necessarily have an equal amount of all three components listed above.

Whilst opinion may vary as to the number of types of ADHD, the DSM lists three main presentations of ADHD at present and it seems to me to be a decent working model. These are as follows:

ADHD - Inattentive presentation (or predominantly inattentive presentation)

This is the diagnosis given when the most prominent symptoms are based around concentration and attention. This was once called ADD, but that diagnosis is not used at present.

ADHD - Hyperactive-Impulsive Presentation (or Predominantly Hyperactive-Impulsive Presentation)

This is the diagnosis given when a person primarily presents as having symptoms around hyperactivity and impulse control but does not present with a sufficient number of the symptoms around concentration and attention.

ADHD - Combined Presentation

This is when a person being diagnosed with ADHD has a sufficient number of symptoms from inattention, hyperactivity and impulse control. This would usually be regarded as the more severe type of ADHD which if left without intervention could potentially cause problems in the life of the developing child.

By now, it is entirely possible that some of us will be recalling certain kids that we have worked with over the years and are formulating questions as to whether there was ever any attempt at formal diagnosis for that child.

Some tips for working with children with ADHD

When working with a young person with the above presentation of ADHD, here are a few tips that you can use to support them with their behaviour.

Behaviour cards

These should ideally be laminated cards. Remember that laminate corners can be surprisingly sharp when cut at 90 degrees into squares so perhaps it is best that the edges are cut into rounds with scissors to prevent any potential accidents.

If the child is unhappy to use this strategy (this could be the case with older children especially) because it makes them stand out you could potentially try a different strategy or modify this so that the cards are somewhere less visible to their peers.

These can have some reminders like

- Raise your hand before asking a question
- Ask before taking a movement break
- Let an adult know if you are struggling

And so forth to reflect the specific needs of the child

Have the day's schedule on display

As simple as that. Have the timetable with timings on display for the children to see. You can discuss what will be happening over the course of the day at the beginning in form time. This may work better with primary aged kids who spend a lot of time in the same class.
If the children are older and you only have them for one or two sessions, it is a good idea to display learning outcomes on the board and perhaps a brief overview of the activities they will be doing.

Be clear of expectations for behaviour

Make sure that there is no ambiguity about the expectations for behaviour in your classroom. You can display these in simple, child friendly terms on the wall somewhere very visible as a reminder to the children. This way they are there to see and the child should not be confused about what is expected of them. You can regularly remind the entire class of the expectations.

Use a points system

A points system can work extremely well in some schools. It is quite surprising how much children will actually buy into a reward points system. Points can be accumulated over the course of a term and can be cashed in at the end of the term for an agreed reward that is meaningful to the child.

The reward must not be cash. This could be used to purchase drugs. The reward should also not be vouchers for well known general online retailers. Often they sell knives and other items which we should not enable children to purchase.

Some examples that have worked well in SEN schools with small classes that I have worked in included but are not restricted to

- A specific pair of trainers or item of clothing
- A specific book or film
- A specific computer game

This way, the reward is actually meaningful to the child and they are motivated to earn points. Alternatively, they could earn points for an end of term trip if there is buy in on this as an activity.

Points could be earned each lesson, for example:

- 1 point for following the classroom rules.
- 1 point for treating those around you with respect.
- 1 point for exceptional effort or extremely good work.

At the end of the lesson you could discuss with the children what points they had earned, if any, and enter these into a spreadsheet or similar system for tracking what the child had earned.

This way, the child is given regular feedback on their positive and negative behaviour and they are motivated to earn points by an agreed reward that is meaningful to them.

I have found this method to work very well with a good many children. A reward points system has helped some unlikely candidates to behave a lot better in class.

At the end of the day it is up to your school if you use something like this, but a £20 item can be a relatively cheap price for the school budget to absorb in return for a child learning to self-moderate their own behaviours.

You can encourage the child to have a picture of what they are working towards taped to their desk as a reminder. This can yield some pretty good results but not everyone will agree with these tactics.

Never pay for items out of your own pocket as that can be interpreted as grooming or similar. This should always be something that the whole school does. The rewards must be agreed as being a reasonable price, age appropriate and the points must be awarded consistently by all staff in order that the system does not cause problems for anyone.

For example, if John the Jazz dance teacher awards Billy 1,000 points for good behaviour, tell them not to do it again and to stick to the plan.

Plan in advance for impulsive behaviours

If your ADHD learner is prone to impulsive behaviours and has not quite learned to pause before acting yet, you really need to have a plan in place for when things go wrong.

When you are planning your lessons, think about potential flashpoints for silly behaviour. What might trigger impulsive behaviour in your learner? What can you do to minimise the risk of this?

You should also try and have some robust strategies in place for distracting and de-escalating the child if they are starting to struggle.

Fiddle toys

You can easily let the ADHD learner have a fiddle toy of some variety on their desk or easily to hand to be given to them. Having something to fiddle with can be of immense benefit to the ADHD learner and physically manipulating some object in their hands is thought to have the following benefits:

- Improving their focus and concentration
- Relieve their feelings of anxiety

- Relieve their feelings of restlessness and boredom
- Help them remain calm and relaxed
- Help reduce fidgeting and the urge to leave their desk or designated area

For example, if there is a spoken part of the lesson where you are explaining some part of a subject or detailing a task to them, a fiddle toy of some variety may help the ADHD learner to remain more focused or even to be less disruptive.

These can either be kept in a box and given out to the learner(s) and collected at the end of the lesson, or if the learner can manage and act responsibly with some manner of fiddle toy, they can carry this around themself.

Whilst opinions on the benefits of fiddle toys for ADHD learners are not unanimous, in my personal opinion, it is a cheap intervention to put in place and some learners report that they find it very helpful for them. Whilst I reserve the right to change my mind, I can't see any harm in this.

A wobble chair is another classroom adaptation to consider. This allows the child to fidget in a focused and non disruptive fashion by wobbling slightly on their chair. If this helps them focus by burning off a little excess energy then it can be a good investment.

In my opinion, a musical instrument is the ultimate fiddle toy for an ADHD kid. If you can get them interested in playing an instrument, it is an amazing thing for them to channel their energy into and also has various benefits for the mental health of the child, although, a child playing bagpipes or accordion randomly in class may not be what you are aiming for.

The egg timer

Some ADHD learners can struggle to maintain focus on a task for extended periods of time. Some learners may respond well to an egg timer or an electronic timer of some variety (or an onscreen timer on the interactive whiteboard). For example, you might negotiate with your learner to work solidly for 5 minutes on a given task and then switch to another task or activity. If they master doing the task for 5 minutes (or whatever you have agreed), then the time can be extended over a period.

Not all learners will respond to this method but some will find the act of *time constraining* a task to be of some benefit to their ability to focus on the task in hand.

Be aware that some egg timers have glass in them and so if a child self-harms or weaponises things, you may want to invest in one without any glass in it.

Seating plan and screens

ADHD learners can be very susceptible to distractions so if you are able to seat your ADHD learner in a spot in the classroom away from distractions, this can potentially be beneficial.

For example, you may try to:

- Sit them away from windows.

- Sit them away from the corridor outside the classroom.
- Sit them away from a particularly talkative peer (or another learner with ADHD).
- Limit visual clutter. Try to keep their immediate environment relatively minimal if possible.
- They may benefit from being seated near to the teacher so that they can ask for help easily if they are struggling.

Consider using a screen if absolutely necessary. Please note that this is not to isolate a child or to prevent them from interacting with their peers. Nor is this in any way, shape, or form punitive or to be used as a punishment, but is simply deployed to reduce distractions around them which they may otherwise find difficult to filter out if they are struggling.

The screen can simply be a thin MDF board or some similar material on a simple stand to give it stability so it is not easily knocked over by an accidental tap. You can easily create a stand using 4 of what are referred to as 'London shelving brackets'.

The screen is simply placed to one side of the learner to reduce distractions. A screen like this can be very cheaply made with parts available at any hardware store. If you have a DT teacher (or another member of staff who is a bit handy), you could ask them if they have the parts laying around to make a couple of these. They may be enthusiastic to help out.

Music on headphones

Some learners with ADHD can find it very helpful to discreetly listen to music or white noise on headphones whilst they are working in order to keep them on task. Of course, this does not mean that they come into the classroom and put their headphones straight on - they will need to follow the lesson just like everyone else will. If they are working on a task and they find it easier to focus with their own music playing, then this is, in my opinion, a reasonable adjustment to make for their learning difference.

Beware letting them play music from YouTube as some learners will just spend the lesson clicking around on YouTube. If it is a playlist and they are focusing on their work then it is not an issue. Free reign on YouTube usually means very little work getting done in my experience.

Equally, beware letting them play music off of their mobile phone as mobiles can cause a lot of issues in the classroom. A recommended method is to let them copy some MP3s to a folder on their computer or laptop and listen from there using software such as VLC player (videolan.org). This is likely to cause the least issues.

This kind of strategy may be difficult to implement in a mainstream school as there may be very strict rules on what can and cannot be done in the classroom and it is not a good idea to undermine the schools rules unless, for example, the SENCO has stated that an exception should be made for a particular learner. Of course, if one child is perceived to be getting preferential treatment by other learners in a mainstream school, this will doubtless be met with a chorus of *'unfair!'* from the rest of the class.

Feedback

Provide regular feedback to the ADHD learner. If they are behaving in a way which meets the standard of your learning space, encourage them, give them praise for this. Equally, if their behaviour is falling short of what can reasonably be expected, let them know swiftly.

Always be consistent in the way that you apply rules and your classroom expectations. This way there is no ambiguity for the learner - they know where they stand and it is easier for them to process and understand what is expected of them.

Support

Now in an ideal world, every child with ADHD would have a member of support staff available to assist them and keep them on track with their tasks whenever they require the additional support. Often in the real world, we would be extremely lucky to have a teaching assistant as well as a teacher in a class of 30 or more. If you have worked in mainstream education you will likely know this to be true.

As such, we rarely have a perfect set up in the classroom to meet the needs of all of our learners. One method that we can employ with an ADHD kid is to pair them up with a learner who can act as a positive influence upon them and help them stay focused.

This must not be to the detriment of the non ADHD child under any circumstances. However, if the child that our ADHD learner is paired with is able to engage in lessons and has spare capacity to help their ADHD peer stay on target then there is no harm in this strategy.

If used with appropriate consideration and planning it can be an extremely useful tool. Under no circumstances should this be used as a substitute for actually interacting with an ADHD learner, interaction and guidance from teacher or teaching assistant is still of primary importance, but a bit of peer support can go a long way if done properly.

Learning outcomes

It can be a positive idea to let your ADHD learners (and all of your learners for that matter) know in a concrete manner what the aim of the lesson is, i.e. what they should be able to do by the end of the lesson or what work they are aiming to complete. This can be displayed on the board at the beginning of the lesson and discussed; there is no harm in the learners copying the learning outcome down in their books or leaving the learning outcome(s) up on the board.

This way the ADHD learner knows what they are aiming for in the lesson. A well-defined and understood target is easier to achieve than a nebulous and poorly defined goal.

3.4 Dyslexia - more information

When opening a discussion about Dyslexia, it can be useful to look at a definition for Dyslexia. There is no single universally agreed definition for Dyslexia, but there are some good starting points that we can use to inform how we think of Dyslexia, what it is and the experience of those people who have Dyslexia and related conditions.

The following does not claim to be a concise definition for dyslexia; rather it is a list of primary facts about Dyslexia, collated from a variety of sources including the BDA, The Rose report and other writers on the subject.

- Dyslexia is considered to be a *neurodevelopmental disorder*. This means that you are born with it, it will emerge early in life, you will have Dyslexia for life. It is likely that it can run in a family and can be inherited by offspring of a Dyslexic person.
- Dyslexia does not affect the level of intelligence that a person has. Many people with Dyslexia are highly intelligent and are very capable in many areas.
- We do not know what causes Dyslexia.
- Dyslexia primarily affects a person's ability in being able to read the written word fluently, i.e. being able to decode this and turn this into meaningful structure. It also primarily affects spelling and the ability to spell. There is more to Dyslexia than this and we will look in more detail shortly.
- Dyslexia can vary in the intensity that it affects a person or how much they are affected in specific areas. Whilst we can generalise about Dyslexia,

individuals will have different strengths and weaknesses.
- Dyslexia is often accompanied by some other symptoms - but these are not specifically considered to be part of the criteria for Dyslexia. These include:

    - Motor skills and coordination
    - The ability to concentrate
    - The ability to self-organise
    - The ability to make mental calculations
    - Difficulties with some aspects of language
    - Visual and Auditory processing difficulties

People with Dyslexia can struggle significantly in some areas and their difficulties can represent a barrier to learning. However, people with Dyslexia are often skilled and talented in other areas of life. Dyslexic people are often highly creative, good at design, excellent at problem solving, spoken language and a variety of other areas.

If suitable interventions are done with Dyslexic learners, ideally from an early age, they can often make good progress depending on the severity of their dyslexia. The relative severity of the Dyslexia can be gauged by the learner's response to structured Dyslexia interventions.

Additionally, there are a wide range of adaptations that can be made in the classroom to make it more inclusive for the Dyslexic learner and this will usually help them further to access education more easily.

It is currently thought that around 1 in 10 people have Dyslexia to a greater or lesser extent and as such, it is my firm belief that every single teacher should make themselves aware of how to make their lessons more accessible to Dyslexic learners as this will help their learners to make progress.

Types of Dyslexia

Firstly, I would like to acknowledge that there is some dispute around how many types of Dyslexia there are (4, 8, 12 etc) and that there is a general lack of consensus on this issue. I do not have an agenda on this debate and as such I will cover the basic varieties as a starting point for your further personal research if you find the study of Dyslexia to be something that you would like to pursue further.

The following 4 types of Dyslexia can be considered subtypes of the main condition. As well as the likely genetic cause for Dyslexia, people can acquire 'Dyslexia' or something that manifests in a very similar way due to brain injury or stroke at any point in their life.

Phonological Dyslexia

Someone with this variety of Dyslexia may well be able to read familiar words that they are used to, but when they come across new words, especially complex words they will experience difficulties. This is the most common type for children to have.

Words as well as being constructed from letters are constructed from phonemes, which are the small sounds which join together to let us know how to say a word.

This aspect of written language is particularly problematic for someone with Phonological Dyslexia and they are likely to significantly struggle with it.

Rapid naming deficit

This variety of Dyslexia, also occasionally known as Rapid Automated Naming (RAN), is a subtype of Dyslexia which causes it to be problematic for a child (or adult) to name a list of things that they have sighted.

For example, if a child with this type of Dyslexia was asked to attach the correct name to each colour that was presented to them on a palette of colours (without accompanying text) they may struggle. There would likely be a delay in them being able to associate the colour that they see with the word that they would recall from their memory. It may take longer to name numbers or letters, so it could be said that this relates to the processing speed of visual information.

Double deficit Dyslexia

Someone with this variety of Dyslexia may struggle significantly. This is a rarer form of Dyslexia where the person will not only experience the difficulties associated with Phonological Dyslexia, but will also experience the difficulties associated with Rapid Naming Deficit. This condition can make progress in reading and writing difficult and can require some specialist intervention.

Surface Dyslexia

Surface Dyslexia can be acquired from brain injury or stroke later in life. Reading words with regular spellings can be manageable, but when words are spelt in an irregular fashion compared to how they are pronounced there can be great difficulty. For example debt, subtle, pretty etc.

Irlens syndrome

It is worth mentioning Irlens syndrome. So far as we know, this is a completely discreet condition from Dyslexia but it can cause difficulties with reading, hence its inclusion in this section. Irlens syndrome is sometimes mistaken for Dyslexia.

Irlens is also sometimes called *visual stress*. It was first identified in the 1980s and is thought to be at least as common as Dyslexia. It would appear that it runs in families (so it is almost definitely hereditary), it affects males and females equally and is usually referred to as *a perceptual processing disorder*.

People who suffer from Irlens are often very sensitive to light and excessive light can cause problems for them, especially when reading for lengths of time. Some of the symptoms that they may experience include

- Eye pain and watering eyes.
- Headaches and migraines when in bright light for a period of time (this includes both fluorescent lights and natural sunlight).
- Visual distortions.

- Fatigue from reading for lengths of time.
- Poor depth perception.
- Attention difficulties (unrelated to ADHD).

Someone with Irlens may find it particularly difficult to read black text on a white background for long periods of time, with this potentially causing their eyes to hurt and/or head ache.

Quite a lot of modern software and computer operating systems have accessibility settings which allow the user/reader to select different colour schemes, which may well make it easier for them to read comfortably. Please make sure that your IT department has not locked users out from changing the accessibility settings on your computers as this could be absolutely vital to some of your learners.

Someone with Dyslexia or Irlens could be allowed to use a laptop or tablet in class in order to help them make the necessary adaptations to be able to read without discomfort. This could easily be written into their personal plan so that staff will know that this is allowed and a reasonable adaptation for such a child.

Screening and assessment

It is important to acknowledge that formal assessment and diagnosis of Dyslexia can only be given by a properly trained and qualified person. If we are not qualified to do this, with a little training, we can use something called a Dyslexia screening tool. This can indicate how likely it may be that a child may have Dyslexia. Whilst this is not a formal diagnosis, it can be used to show a need for further, formal investigation.

There are a wide variety of screening tools available, some free, some paid for. Some of these will be an electronic system on a computer, some will be paper based. They will sometimes include a list of various criteria relating to the child and their ability which a teacher and SENCO may be best placed to fill out most of. There are a variety of different screening tools available and a search engine will enable you to find hundreds of varying quality. It is not a bad idea to talk to the SENCO and see if your school has something already purchased or already in use as there is no point in reinventing the wheel.

Assistive technology

There is a wide range of assistive technology for dyslexic learners that can help them in a range of tasks that they may otherwise struggle with. The landscape of which software is 'the best' at any given time shifts around and software is often released in updated versions with new features.
Assistive software tends to fall into the following categories although, of course, some pieces of software will have capabilities in more than one of these areas. If you are tasked with choosing assistive software for your classroom or school, you will have to do a phase of research and see what your budget can stretch to, or if there is freeware that might do the job for your learners and/or Dyslexic adult team members.

Speech recognition software

This type of software will in theory, recognise what words are spoken to it and convert them into text in a word processing document. Some amazing advances have been made in this area, but I will offer the disclaimer that the results can be dependent on how clearly the user speaks and the degree of background noise present. Speech recognition software can sometimes make some strange and occasionally comical judgements over what has been said. Some are better than others. Text created this way will always need a proof read before going 'out into the wild'. It is possible to invest in a highly directional microphone for use with this type of software if background chatter is an issue.

Text to Speech software

This type of software will basically read to the Dyslexic learner from text in a written document. The voices generated by this type of software used to be sometimes jarring and robotic, but they often sound more natural in modern software. This could discreetly be used by a learner on headphones who struggles with reading.

Mind Mapping Software

This type of software allows Dyslexics (and other learners with SEN) to plan their work more effectively and can be a great help in making a task less confusing to complete.

Spell checkers

We are all likely familiar with this type of software which usually comes as a standard basic feature of word processing software. It can be very useful for a Dyslexic learner to get into the habit of using this feature in order to correct difficult spellings.

Reading pens

These allow a learner to run the device over an area of text and it will read it to them. This will work best with standard fonts and a steady hand.

Smart pens

This is a more modern innovation which tracks the handwritten notes of the learner and converts them into digital format and uploads them to somewhere such as a laptop or mobile phone, for later use.

The standard classroom adaptation

If you have not already read this chapter, you should go and do so. This is a standard classroom adaptation that you should start to use, which includes some features that will probably make accessing learning easier for your Dyslexic learners as well as other learners with SpLDs or SEN.

3.5 Attachment and attachment disorder

In this section we will be having a relatively brief look at the fairly deep topic of attachment theory. Attachment theory itself is widely recognised as having been developed by a British psychologist called John Bowlby in the latter half of the 20th century. Since its creation, his theory of attachment has become broadly accepted and is now used as a standard model.

Attachment, as used in the field of psychology (and associated fields) means *'a lasting psychological connectedness between two human beings'*. In this context, attachment theory is concerned with a process that happens in very early childhood between child and their primary caregiver. Stereotypically the primary caregiver might be their mother, but this is not always the case and their primary caregiver could equally be their father or grandparent, for example. Children can also form attachments with multiple caregivers.

An emotional bond is formed over time with the primary caregiver(s) through regular and healthy interaction and this helps for the child to develop in a healthy and emotionally secure style. This is called *secure attachment*.

If there is some kind of disruption to the secure attachment process, this can result in difficulties in the child's development which can cause problems for them which can persist into adult life. Some attachment issues that arise from early childhood experiences can be minimised by appropriate therapy.

In order for secure attachment to develop, the primary caregiver or caregivers must not neglect the needs of the child and they must be attuned to what the child needs and when. They must also be consistent in their behaviour. For example, they must be able to recognise when the child is hungry and meet that need; recognise when the child simply wants to interact and meet that need; recognise when the child needs personal care and to meet that need.

Sometimes a primary caregiver can fail in this or be prevented from meeting the basic needs of the child. This may be through no fault of their own, for example if they have mental health problems or are the victim of domestic violence. Sometimes a child requires intensive care directly after birth to keep them alive, this strange environment and restricted access to a primary caregiver could cause them to develop attachment difficulties. Other reasons could be drug and alcohol abuse by the parent, illness, bereavement of a primary caregiver, if they are in care from an early age there may be several changes of caregiver, or various other things. Factors such as these can lead to secure attachment not happening in the child's development.

The most critical phase of the attachment process happens in the first two years of the child's life. In order for this to happen healthily, the primary caregivers need to be available, creating a stable environment and to meet the needs of the child. Attachment starts to happen properly around 6 weeks into life.

All being well, attachment should be strong around the 6 months mark, with the child showing 'separation anxiety', when they are separated from their primary caregiver(s).

Between 18 months to 2 years in their development, the child will begin the process of becoming less dependent on the primary caregiver and will begin to explore the world around them a little more, especially if they feel secure in their attachment and that their primary caregiver is reliable in their support and that the caregiver will return predictably if they are out of sight briefly.

Due to this process of forming an attachment (or lack thereof) with a primary caregiver, the first two years of life are particularly crucial in creating a healthy foundation for the child to grow from. The process of attachment in these first two years can affect the child throughout their childhood and adult life.

Secure attachment has a profound effect on the development of the child, in a variety of ways. The child is likely to develop prosocial behaviours, the ability to interact with their peers more healthily, self-confidence and various other attributes.

Secure attachment even alters the physical development of the brain. The regular healthy interaction and the needs of the child being properly met gives rise to healthy brain development and all that goes with it. Conversely, neglect and trauma in the early years can cause the development of the brain to be hindered.

If secure attachment has not happened for the child, it can profoundly affect things such as the following, all the way through adulthood

- Their ability to trust people.
- Their feelings of self-worth.

- Their sense of self confidence in interacting with other people.
- The way that they view relationships.
- The way that they view themself.
- Their ability to parent well.
- Their ability to maintain healthy relationships.
- Behavioural difficulties.
- Poor mental health.

The attachment styles

There are generally agreed to be 4 main attachment styles. In practice, you will actually see these written in a variety of different ways as the convention for naming the 4 attachment styles does not seem to be standardised.

Most variations on the naming of these will very likely contain the same basic 4 words, namely secure, avoidant, ambivalent and disorganised. For the purposes of this discussion we will refer to them as

- Secure attachment
- Avoidant attachment
- Ambivalent attachment
- Disorganised attachment

Avoidant and ambivalent attachment styles may be considered less than ideal, but it is only disorganised attachment which strongly constitutes an *attachment disorder*.

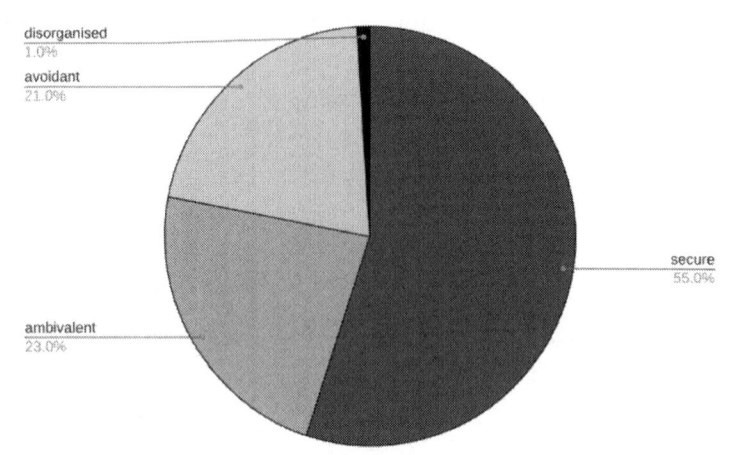

The above is reasonably representative of attachment styles in the general population. Different studies have yielded slightly different results.
Only around 55% of people have 'secure attachment'.

You may well see the phrase *attachment disorder* come up in connection with some of the children that you work with. This may be more or less common, depending on the type of school that you work at.

If they have been properly assessed by a professional (such as an educational psychologist), there should hopefully be a report which will give you some details and recommendations about their attachment style and perhaps some ideas about how to best work with them.

It is important to note that not everyone purely has one attachment style and there can be an overlap of styles or someone can change attachment style over the course of their life.

It is also very important to note that attachment disorder can easily be mistaken for conditions such as ADHD (and

ODD) and Autism, but has a very different cause. Given this, I would advise avoiding attempting armchair diagnosis of Attachment Disorder too much. If you have concerns, speak to your SENCO, but it is really the job of a highly skilled professional to tell the difference between attachment and other kinds of SEN.

We will now look at the 4 attachment styles in turn.

Secure attachment

It is reckoned that over half of the population has the secure attachment style.

This is the attachment style that develops when the child has had at least one primary caregiver who has met their basic needs and interacted with them in a consistent and caring way throughout the first two years of their life. This style of attachment is referred to as being *organised*.

The word *'Organised'* is used to describe some of the attachment styles because the child has developed an *organised strategy* in response to a reasonable predictability from their primary caregiver and environment and they know what to do.

A child that has secure attachment is more likely to interact with their peers in a healthy way, have a healthy attitude to danger, have good self-esteem, have healthy relationships, share their feelings with partners and friends and seek out social support as appropriate.

This style of attachment is considered to be the ideal attachment style and tends to give rise to the happiest children and adults, based on the pervasive influence of their early childhood.

In the classroom, a child with this attachment style may often appear to be content and engaged in their work; they will often be sociable and able to work independently or in group without difficulty. A child with this attachment style *may* be less likely to present you with challenging behaviour in general.

Avoidant attachment

It is reckoned that somewhere approaching a quarter of the population has this attachment style. This does not mean that those people are mentally ill, simply that they do not have what is usually considered to be the ideal attachment style.

This style of attachment is referred to as being *organised* because there is a degree of predictability in the parental behaviour and as such the child will organise their behaviour patterns to accommodate for this.

This style of attachment tends to develop when a parent behaves in a specific way towards the child. They may

- Minimise the feelings of the child.
- Ridicule the child.
- Refuse to meet the demands or needs of the child.
- Refuse to help them with difficult tasks or tasks that the child finds difficult.
- Could be described as cold and distant in their parenting style.

As the child develops, they learn that the primary caregiver is not very approachable and not always helpful towards them. Their attachment style organises around this principle and they become *avoidant* in their insecure attachment.

In a child this will usually appear as the following group of behaviours:

- They may avoid their parents or primary care givers.
- They do not seek much comfort or safety from their parent(s) or primary caregiver.
- They have no real preference between their primary caregiver and complete strangers.

Contrast this with the secure attachment style where a young child will see their primary caregiver as a safe base of operations to explore the world from and seek them out for comfort at such times when they require it.

The child with avoidant attachment also poses a specific risk to themself as their willingness to interact with strangers, even under potentially dangerous circumstances makes them potentially open to exploitation and abuse.

If you are working with a child with this attachment style, you should carefully risk assess any activities which they participate in out in the community, in order to reduce the risks to them as much as possible. Planning to reduce risk can include something as simple as having a designated adult who is named in the risk assessment as having the responsibility for keeping such a child in line of sight whilst out in the community.

In the classroom, this type of child may be very much focused on their own needs and they may ignore the needs of others around them. They would probably be a child that needs their personal space more than others.

If a child with this attachment style becomes stuck in their work, they would usually not seek (or may be reluctant) to ask for help from an adult and so they may struggle with a piece of work that they do not understand until through frustration they tear up their work, become distressed, are unable to complete their work or something similar.

Because of their underlying distrust for adults stemming from their experiences in early childhood from their primary caregiver (which they are possibly completely unaware of) they will often not seek the assistance of adults and will seek to do things by themself or not at all.

A child with this attachment style may develop into an adult who has difficulties in maintaining relationships, difficulty in sharing their emotions and they may not invest much emotion into their relationships.

Ambivalent attachment

It is thought that somewhere in the region of 20% of the population have this attachment style. This style of attachment is also referred to as being *organised* because the child has organised their behaviour patterns to accommodate for parental behaviour from their early years.

The ambivalent attachment style tends to develop when a parent is inconsistent in their emotional availability, emotional response and care for a child during their early years. They may be emotionally responsive to the child on one day and completely ignore them the next. This leaves the child feeling confused, insecure, distrustful and ambivalent toward the primary caregiver(s).

A child with this attachment style will often have very low self-esteem and may have a very negative view of themself. They may also have a strong fear of rejection.

In the classroom, they may actively want the attention of the adult/teacher, so they work out ways to get attention. Sometimes the methods they develop to get attention from the adult are not positive and they may have some difficulty telling the difference between positive and negative attention, unconsciously working to the principle that *'all attention is good attention'*.

They may behave in a way which is against the expectations for their behaviour in class, simply in order to get the attention that they crave. Remember that this is due to early childhood experiences that were beyond their control. In effect, they would rather be getting told off in class than to feel that they are not being noticed by the adult.

A child with ambivalent attachment may also not be particularly interested in formal reward systems and points based systems that may work fairly well for the rest of the class. You can, of course, negotiate a meaningful reward for that child that motivates them if your school allows for this type of approach.

In the classroom, a child with this attachment style may present as being insecure and anxious. They may seek reassurance on a basis which is far more regular than might be considered 'average'. Their need for reassurance can make them overly dependent on the teacher and they may ask questions to which they already know the answers stemming from feelings of insecurity that they may have.

A child with this attachment style may also be very quick to blame their peers or the teacher for anything which goes wrong, even when this is something that they may have done themself. A child with ambivalent attachment may struggle to maintain friendships with their peers which can lead them to be socially isolated.

As an adult, people with this attachment style can have great difficulties trusting their partner, even if their partner is trustworthy. They may suffer from depression and other mental health issues.

Disorganised attachment

Somewhere around 1% of the population is thought to have this attachment style. It is sometimes called reactive attachment or RAD, but for the purposes of this chapter, we will call it disorganised attachment.

This style of attachment is what we would consider to be proper *attachment disorder* and we may sometimes see it linked with the name of a child who we work with, depending on where we work.

Contrasted to the previous 3 attachment styles which are considered to be 'organised', this attachment style is considered to be disorganised.

This is because the parent or primary caregiver's responses and behaviours towards the child were unpredictable in the first two years of their life. As such, the child does not develop a consistent or *organised* approach/strategy to the parent and life. Their attachment style is disorganised, caused by the potential chaos and unpredictability of their early experiences of life and their primary caregiver.

Often with the disorganised attachment style there will have been accompanying factors that will have pervaded the child's early years. These will often be difficulties such as *physical, emotional or sexual abuse, neglect and trauma*. Interaction with the parent may well cause feelings of fear in the child. This can cause considerable confusion and angst for the child.

If the child was not the subject of the abuse themself, then they may have been a witness, perhaps regularly, to the abuse occurring. Often there will have been uncertainty as to whether their basic needs would be met or not. Their early years would likely have been filled with uncertainty and fear and probably neglect.

When a child has this attachment style, it can, but does not always, result in some fairly extreme behaviours. The desire to control the people around them can be a key factor in this attachment style.

In children, you may see:

- Controlling and manipulative behaviour.
- They insist on things being on their own terms or not at all.
- They can be very controlling to their peers and the adults around them.
- Controlling people can make them feel more secure and safe.
- They may view the world as a particularly hostile and unfriendly place.

If you are working with a child who has disorganised attachment in your classroom or in your school, you may find that internally, they have very low self-esteem and feelings of self-hate. Based on their predisposition from early childhood, they will often view the world as fraught with danger and adults as being potential sources of danger, specifically so towards them.

You may find that their mood can swing like a pendulum although this is not always the case. The child with disorganised attachment in your class may be very depressed at times, very angry at times and may also be particularly defiant towards you. They may well have difficulties around emotional dysregulation and may feel at the mercy of their own emotions, which they may experience so strongly, they struggle to control them.

Here are a few pointers for working with a child with disorganised attachment/ attachment disorder:

- You will probably need to put in the ground work to make friends with a child with this condition. This may take time as it is possible that they do not trust adults or their motivations at all. You will simply have to be patient and put in the groundwork with this kind of child. If you have a friendly relationship with them, with time, they may grow to trust you somewhat and may be less inclined towards hostile behaviour.

- As this type of child with attachment disorder can be quite controlling, offer them choices rather than giving them orders. You can of course work to the principle that *'all roads lead to Rome'* and give them choices relating to what you would ideally like them to do, but giving them even the illusion of control may help to minimise incidents.
- Be reliable. The adults in their life may not have demonstrated this quality consistently or positively. Break that pattern and be consistent in your behaviour and reliable to the child. If you say you are going to do something - do it, if humanly possible.
- Recognise those early warning signs that this child is getting anxious or agitated and do your best to redirect them. Develop some strategies for distracting them or de-escalating them. More on this in the next chapter

3.6 Behavioural difficulties and de-escalation techniques

As lovely as the children that we work with are, there will be times that they may get into a *heightened state*. This means that something has triggered them and they are either becoming seriously unsettled or are already there.

The end result of this can be some negative and undesirable behaviour that is best avoided through modifying the way we interact and behave around the child.

However, for all of our efforts to maintain a calm and fun space for the children to work, grow and learn in, sometimes things can go awry for reasons that are beyond our control. This is when we need to use *de-escalation techniques*.

Before we delve into de-escalation techniques, let us first look at what happens when the child is somehow triggered and what is happening within the child's mind during a heightened episode.

Some children will accelerate more rapidly from the initial trigger or cause of upset, to a state of being extremely heightened or reaching meltdown. This will vary from one child to another. I have worked with some children who can progress from their baseline normal mood to extreme anger *very* rapidly and others who have shifted from one state to another far more slowly in a more predictable fashion.

If you know the child, it is always best to try and avoid triggering them at all and if this does happen to recognise the early warning signs that all is not well.

Generally after experiencing something that has triggered the child, they will express some manner of agitation. This can manifest differently in different children. Try and learn what these early signs look like and do something to de-escalate them at this point to avoid them entering a more serious state and potentially having some real difficulties.

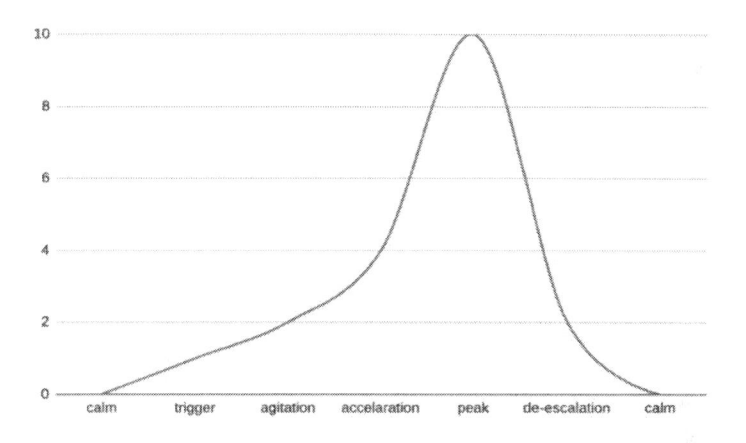

This diagram shows how an event usually unfolds for a child. During the peak phase, they may become violent, unresponsive, self-harm or vandalise property. This is very dependent on the individual child.

If we were to look at what is happening inside the brain of the child who is entering a heightened state, as depicted on the graph above, we would see certain things occurring. This book is not intended to be an in depth guide to the human brain, the information offered here is intended to give a general idea of what is happening to a child who has entered a heightened state.

The 'thinking' part of the brain is physically located at the front of the brain. This deals with our higher reasoning, problem solving and executive functions. This is the part of the brain where the more rational thinking takes place. This is the section of your mind that deals with cool and calm decision making. We call this the *prefrontal cortex*.

Next to this we have the *midbrain*. This is the part of the brain where emotions are experienced. It also relates to memory and regulating behaviours. This is also referred to as the *Limbic system*.

Behind this we have the rear brain. This is a more primitive part of the brain that deals with things like survival and fight or flight responses that can arise as a result of adverse stimulus, threats or perceived threats. This is also referred to as the *brain stem and amygdala*.

When a child gets into a heightened state (as seen at the peak stage of the graph on the previous page) from a real or perceived threat or becomes sufficiently upset about something, often the fight or flight response will kick in.

When this happens, the rear brain, (the brain stem and amygdala) takes over as this is the part of the brain which governs the fight or flight response. At this time, the forebrain is disengaged and so the capacity for rational thought is diminished or absent. This will continue until the child has managed to de-escalate from their heightened state.

At this point, the child's brain will be flooded with Cortisol and Adrenaline making it difficult for them to actually reason.

In practice, this means that if a child is experiencing a heightened state there are a few things that you need to do or not do. These are as follows.

- Attempting to reason with them may actually make things worse if the rational part of their mind is disengaged because they are at the peak of an episode. Once they start to de-escalate a little from the peak you may be able to reason with them.
- Remain calm. If you become highly agitated yourself, it is only likely to prolong the episode.
- Do not raise your voice as this may exacerbate the episode.
- Do not make demands on the child such as *'calm down', 'stop this instantly'*. The likelihood of this being an effective tactic when they have reached peak is minimal as they are not in a state where they are reasoning very well.
- Do not crowd their personal space - they may be more likely to lash out at you if you crowd them. If a child is about to harm themselves or other children, of course, you have a duty to intervene but if they are raging, give them a little space if safe to do so.
- You may need to remove other children from the classroom or space that you are in. There could be a plan in place for how this happens if the child frequently goes into meltdown, for example, your trusted TA could take the other kids out into the corridor whilst the episode unfolds or a quick walk around the block. Whatever is deemed most appropriate for your setting.

Physical intervention

Some schools will have a policy around physical interventions, which means the adults are trained to physically hold a child when they are in a heightened state. This should only be done after staff have attended a proper training course delivered by a qualified instructor in one of the systems that teach how to do this safely such as team teach or TCI (Therapeutic Crisis Intervention).

If you have not completed such training, you should only get involved in a physical situation in order to prevent harm coming to someone and then use the absolute minimum possible force. You can easily injure a child, so play it safe.

From a legal perspective, physical holds can be used for the following reasons:

- To prevent a child from hurting themself
- To prevent a child from hurting others
- To prevent a child from damaging property
- To prevent a child from causing disorder

Whilst most people can imagine scenarios where we might have to hold a child to prevent them from injuring themself or doing serious harm to someone, the last of these four justifications for physical intervention is extremely vague and broad. In my opinion, this can be used as an ad hoc justification for completely unnecessary physical interventions and if you are using this to justify why you are holding children, you are on very shaky territory.

I strongly disapprove of teaching (or care) staff who are too eager to perform physical interventions. There are occasions where this has to happen for reasons of safety but generally it is a very poor way to manage the behaviours of most children and it is not a good way to cope with things that may happen in school.

Real skill and wisdom lies in knowing the child and recognising when they are struggling *before they hit the point of meltdown* and doing something non-invasive before an incident develops.

If some of the staff where you work seem to spend half of their lives on the floor holding down crying children, this is an immense red flag which should not be ignored as this can easily become a form of abuse directed towards the children.

Many years ago, I ran a school which was part of a group of schools for children with challenging behaviour. The statistics for serious incidents were very low for this school and the levels of physical intervention were correspondingly very low. I was asked by someone high up in the company if my team and I were reporting things properly - I could honestly confirm that we were.

I was asked by colleagues what was being done to facilitate this miraculously low number of physical interventions. My simple answer was: *'Noticing when the child is unhappy and talking to them or de-escalating them before things get out of hand'.*

I do not regard this as rocket science and it is something that you should strive for too if humanly possible. We will now look at some practical techniques.

Ways that we can de-escalate before hitting crisis point

There are many simple methods that we can embed into our own behaviour towards the children, which are both healthy and useful. After all, hopefully none of us wants to see a child in an advanced state of distress and this is quite often avoidable. We should ideally be striving to avoid children getting into a heightened state but of course, it is not always possible to avert this from happening.

If you are getting a handover about the child, then pay attention to it; if the handover is vague, ask for it to be clarified. If the child is having a very hard time outside of school for one reason or another, this may make them more prone to getting into a heightened state, i.e. their fuse may be shorter than usual. If you are forearmed with the knowledge that something is happening for them, take extra care. Do a check in with them when they arrive, give them a space to unload their woes if they feel inclined to do so.

If a child appears to have been triggered and is getting into the agitation stage

- Try giving them two or three positive choices instead of directly telling them what to do. The positive choices that you offer will depend on your setting and the child, but there is usually something that can be offered. For example, *'Would you like to go for a five minute walk with the TA?'* or, *'Would you like to do a different activity for five minutes?'* or, *'Would you like to help me do some jobs around*

the classroom and have a chat?'. The answer might be a flat no, but it is worth a try.
- If the child is getting agitated specifically by you, see if you can facilitate a change of face for a few minutes. Get another adult to work with them for a little bit if possible. See if this helps them de-escalate before things get more problematic.
- If a specific activity seems to be agitating them, if possible, see if you can change activity for a little bit. Whilst this *might not be on the lesson plan*, having a major incident in class hopefully is not either and it may well be the lesser of evils if some heightened behaviour can be avoided.
- Get down to the child's level. Don't loom over them as this could quicken their journey to fight or flight by making them feel threatened. Keep your tone of voice friendly to neutral and try to be on the same eye level as them.
- If the child clearly doesn't want to interact with you, it may be as simple as saying *'I will come back in a couple of minutes'* and simply giving them a bit of breathing space. Obviously you would be keeping a vigilant eye out from a distance just in case something serious is brewing. I have known a few fierce children to react incredibly well to just giving them a few moments to calm themselves a little with less stimulation.
- Distract them. Sometimes the child may be snapped out of it by your doing something to create a distraction and hopefully a change in direction for their train of thought or feelings. This can mean many different things. You could hand them a stuffed toy, tell them a terrible joke, juggle, play noughts and crosses. Ask their advice about

something. Be creative, know the child and see if there is a way that you can avert a crisis by thinking outside of the box a little.
- Don't be judgemental or critical. Even if the child has said something unpleasant to you or has wound you up a little, remember that you are the adult in the situation and behave as such. Do not respond with sarcasm or by telling them *'this is the fifth time this week you have gotten wound up, when are you going to grow up?'* or some similar barb. This will do exactly nothing to make the situation better and will be extremely likely to simply pour petrol on the already smouldering fire. Stand your ground but be calm and polite. Model the behaviour you would like the child to develop.
- If you know the child and you have had a chance to do some deep breathing exercises, such as taught in one of the appendices of this book, take some time out to do this with them. This will help lower their heart rate, potentially shut down upsetting thoughts and slow the release of stress hormones in their brain. Not every child will be willing or able to learn and participate in this, but, you may be extremely surprised to find that many of the kids that you work with are willing to learn a new technique such as this. It is something you could even try to do with them at the start of the day as part of your routine. This technique *does work* and has long lasting benefits for the person who gets into the habit of doing it regularly.
- Pick your battles wisely. If something that you are doing or insisting upon is getting a child agitated, consider to yourself, *is this really worth sending the child completely over the edge over?* Sometimes

the answer may be yes, for example if they are bullying another child or racially abusing someone, but the vast majority of the time the answer is going to be no. Consider if a small change in direction, even for just a few minutes, is worth a try in order to avert a crisis.
- If the child is misbehaving to get your attention, you could consider giving them your undivided attention for a couple of minutes. This may do the trick.

I repeat - Intervene early, as soon as you see the warning signs that the child is getting agitated. You may save the child from some extreme distress and prevent the whole class from being disrupted. Think smart with de-escalation.

3.7 Therapeutic practice

A strange thing I have noticed over the years is that when I have spoken to various people who work in education or around the edges of it, is that when I have stated that I work in SEN and sometimes with behaviourally challenged young people, they have stated something along the lines of *'you must be really good at crowd control and discipline'* - Wrong.

I have always worked in a manner which is *therapeutic* rather than being gifted with the world's loudest voice. This isn't to say that I cannot adopt a tone of voice which can stop the average teenager frozen in their tracks at 20 paces, but this is very rarely the first tool which I reach for when working with young people. Like most things, a loud voice has its place in our tool kits, but it should generally not be the first tool that we reach for in our interactions - it will become ineffective with overuse and it is seldom an efficient way to soothe a child and to get them to sit back down and interact in a more calm way.

Therapeutic practice describes a different model of interaction that you may or may not already be aware of. A good few schools I have known over the years describe themselves as being *'therapeutic'* and their staff as being *'therapeutic practitioners'* but the truth is that this is not always the case and is sometimes simply a selling point to put on promotional literature. There is often a folder detailing the training staff have had to be *'therapeutic practitioners'* but little more, let alone a consistent demonstration of therapeutic practice in their actions.

Therapeutic practice is more a way of interacting with the children you work with. We find that some people are naturally therapeutic in their approach and others have to learn to model this type of behaviour. There are several different models of therapeutic working with children but they tend to come down to relatively similar things under closer scrutiny.

Most commonly, therapeutic practice is employed with children who have suffered Adverse Childhood Experiences (ACE's), have attachment disorder or have suffered trauma. I have seen it be beneficial to a good many different types of children and may produce good results and progress for them too.

What is it then? A school which is therapeutic will generally teach the usual academic subjects as prescribed by the DfE, with the usual attention to add ons such as SMSC and British Values.

In addition to the standard offer, a therapeutic school will have a strong emphasis on the children's mental health and emotional well-being and the children's development in these areas.

When done properly, this will be a whole school approach which in theory is reflected in the practice of all staff. Often, a therapeutic school will have an in house counsellor or therapist of some variety who will do sessions with the children as necessary.

There will generally be regular meetings between education staff and therapeutic staff to discuss the needs and progress of the children and to discuss what approach is best suited to the individual child's needs and what is working and what is not. If a staff team engages in this properly, it can be an extremely useful way of regrouping, thinking about things differently, aligning practice and discussing things collectively.

In some settings, where there are children in care or a school is attached to a specific children's care home or group of care homes, a representative from care will be a part of these meetings, as well as education and therapy. This is sometimes referred to as a triangulated approach.

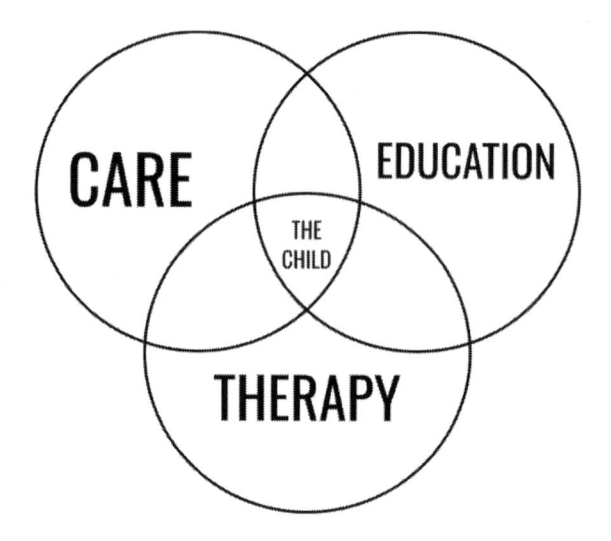

CARE EDUCATION THE CHILD THERAPY

Ideally in such triangulated meetings, there will be equal input from all of the professionals involved but this is not always the case, sometimes with one corner of the triangle attempting to dominate the direction that such planning takes, for example if residential care attempts to tell the school how they should be delivering subjects or if the school attempts to tell the care staff what the children should be having for dinner in the evening. Whilst everyone should have a good level of input, there should also be respect for each team's specialised knowledge.

The general idea behind this type of approach is that if all of the people in a therapeutic setting are working to the same plan and the same set of strategies and targets for the children, they are more likely to have positive results. Ideally the professionals should all be pulling in the same direction and should be working hand in hand as child centred practitioners, in a cooperative and ego free manner.

There are various models for therapeutic practice. One which is fairly commonly used in the UK, at the time of writing, is PACE (Formerly called PLACE).

PACE methodology was developed by an American psychologist called Dr Dan Hughes who worked with children who had Adverse Childhood Experiences (ACE), had suffered trauma and may have attachment issues.

Children who have experienced ACE may have difficulties feeling safe and may be very distrustful of adults, which from their life experiences may well make complete sense, if we look at it from their perspective. This can make it difficult for them to engage in ways which we might regard as typical for children of their age.

PACE stands for:
- Playfulness
- Acceptance
- Curiosity
- Empathy

Playfulness is concerned with the attitude that you take to the children in your interactions. To engage with them on a level that is friendly and even fun. This way the child may grow to enjoy being around you. This makes it easier to interact with them and even sometimes to deliver a message which may not be well received, such as a discussion about something which has gone wrong or a behaviour which was not ideal.

Acceptance is the concept of accepting the child as they are and accepting their emotions which can sometimes be extreme or seem irrational, unpredictable and dysregulated to the observer. This does not mean unconditionally accepting questionable behaviour which can be challenged in a supportive and friendly fashion. Even though from your perspective, the child's interpretation of the world around them might seem at odds with your perception of it, accept that this is their legitimate experience at that time and try to gently explore it with them.

Curiosity means to take an interest in exploring what is happening for the child and what is going on in their life. It can also mean to take an interest in what the child has to say about their feelings and to simply listen. Take an interest in them, listen to what they are saying and you will hopefully build a bond with that child and better understand them and therefore be in a better position to help them.

Empathy is simply put, showing that you care in a non-judgemental fashion. Show that you empathise with what the child is experiencing in the way that you speak to and interact with the child. If the child expresses a negative feeling to you, you do not necessarily have to correct the child and tell them that they are wrong; this could even be throwing petrol on the fire by doing so. You could just express that you are sorry to hear the child feels that way and encourage them to explore what they are expressing. Put yourself in the child's shoes; consider their life experiences so far as you are aware of them and think about how this has affected them.

Using a methodology such as PACE can help reduce the child's feelings of anxiety and their feelings that they are fundamentally unsafe. These feelings are often perfectly reasonable for them to have based on their past life experiences. It is your job as the professional to help the child to see that they are in a safe and accepting environment with people who care about their wellbeing.

Other than the benefit of the child's levels of wellbeing improving and there hopefully being a positive impact on their mental health in general, the application of PACE may lead to less problematic behaviour in the school.

I can give you a relevant example here. Many years ago I went to work at a school for SEN children out in the countryside; within this school there were several classes where the most 'behaviourally challenged' children were somewhat cordoned off. I was presented with what were considered to be the most behaviourally challenged and aggressive children in the school.

I think this was largely due to no other member of staff particularly wanting to engage with them, which is quite sad really considering that these were people who had chosen to work in such a setting.

This very small class of only three children had some behaviours which were in all fairness quite dangerous. These included assaulting staff with improvised weapons and hitting each other, which despite their *just* pre-teen age, could be quite concerning. There were also some problematic sexualised behaviours to add to the concerns around these kids.

At the time of my entering the scene, the main tool used to moderate the children's behaviour was physical restraint, with one of the children specifically, spending up to half of each school day being held down on a couch, which was conveniently positioned just outside of the classroom.

Two fully grown adults would immobilise the child at the first sign of trouble and then the child would scream, cry and would attempt to bite or spit on the adults as they were pinned in place and often verbally berated for their behaviour. This was even written into the school's plan for 'caring' for this child.

Needless to say, I was highly concerned (horrified in fact) with this and could not see any long term benefit to these children from reinforcing their feelings of distrust for adults and even reinforcing that adults are going to physically hurt them.

Luckily, I was in a position where I could start to redirect the team of TA's who I was leading in the classroom. At this point there was nearly 2:1 staffing for the children to physically manage their behaviours. A more enlightened approach would make this unnecessary.

If you come across a school whose main strategy for behaviour management is to throw increasingly large numbers of staff (flooding) at misbehaving children, I would regard this as a red flag around their competency.

If in staff meetings you hear the grumbling cry of, 'we could manage this situation if we had another ten burly members of staff to patrol the school' or 'we need another two TA's in each classroom and an additional ten classrooms to physically restrain misbehaving children in', ask yourself this:

Are these the real challenges at play? Could it be the adults who are working with the children who are at fault and that they need to reassess their strategies for managing children's behaviour?

A difficult and potentially unpopular question to ask perhaps. Reflecting on the possible shortcomings in our own practice or those of our colleagues can be uncomfortable to consider and may even bruise the egos of some adults who have become entrenched in very poor practice.

Some adults may even seem to gain a sense of satisfaction from physically restraining children - if you come across this behaviour, please be aware that it is a form of abuse. Report it to people higher up in your organisation such as the DSL or head. If your DSL or head is part of the problem, I would speak to the local authority for advice. The virtual school or the child's social worker could equally be starting points for an investigation. Anyway, back to the story.

After observing the questionable practice, I called a meeting with the squad of TAs in my class and discussed a new way of working with the children. One of the TAs was particularly ill disposed towards any change in their practice and perhaps luckily for everyone else spent most of their time chit chatting with their friend who was one of the managers, in their office, away from the classroom. This was to be completely frank, no hardship for anyone.

Some of the changes I suggested that we implement were not dissimilar to the PACE methodology I discussed previously but were delivered as some practical techniques that we would employ in the classroom from that point onward.

One completely crucial method was for the staff to learn to recognise when the child was starting to become distressed by observing the early warning signs, taking a step back and remaining calm as we engaged with the child. As simple as it sounds this was in stark contrast to what was being done previously, i.e. raising the voice and moving in ready to restrain at the first sign of trouble, which would yield depressingly predictable results.

There were various other therapeutic measures put in place such as some emotional literacy work, mindfulness and target setting for the children. Target setting was done with a trusted staff member and the child. The child would be encouraged to reflect with the member of staff about what both staff and child could do differently and then the child and staff member would work towards this.

We implemented short and focused twice daily meetings before the children arrived on site to discuss any information we had about the children's well-being (e.g. if they had had a bad night previously or were due contact with a problematic parent if they were in care) and anything in particular that was happening that day and who would be doing what etc.

After the children had left, we would have another short and focused meeting where we would reflect on what had gone well and what had not, how we might modify our approach and what we needed to do the following day.

Lines of communication were established with the carers or care homes of the children to share information and to give feedback about what had gone well and what had not. This way we could be advised ahead of a child arriving if they were in an emotionally difficult place and we could plan accordingly. If child 'A' had had a horrendous night, we might plan to start the day with a light activity that could get them into a better state of mind before we go into the maths lesson.

It was a somewhat flexible approach, but we still had a strong focus on academic activities to meet their educational needs, just as you would expect to find in any mainstream school. It is important to remember that regardless of whether you are a therapeutic school or not, you are still a school and should be teaching proper, meaningful lessons rather than just doing colouring in and board games all day.

What was the impact of this shift in approach? We found that not only could we casually observe the following but could also prove from the data we were gathering that:

- The incidents of physical intervention being required dramatically fell and dwindled to being very infrequent. We had the *'restraint sofa'* removed and banished to the staff room where it remained.
- The incidents of dangerous behaviour amongst the children dramatically fell, such as assaulting staff, destroying the classroom, running from the classroom to be pursued and then restrained by staff.
- The children engaged in classroom work far more than they had previously and started to make measurable academic progress in their learning as well as actually seeming to enjoy their lessons.

We also implemented things like various lunchtime clubs where the children could optionally stay in for a part of lunch time to eat their packed lunches if they wanted to (especially when it was raining) and do an agreed activity such as arts and crafts, watching an agreed TV show with an appropriate tone, reading comics or something of this ilk. The activity would be agreed between children using the following skills which they needed assistance in developing:

- Discussion with their peers which had to be of a respectful tone.
- The participants being allowed turns to speak (turn taking).
- Compromise on the agreed activity if there was disagreement, which could sometimes involve more than one activity being done but in an agreed order that would have to be negotiated by the kids. They got skilled at negotiating and compromising

incredibly rapidly as they learnt that this was a way that they could all get to do something that they enjoyed.

We used a wide variety of strategies like this and found the results to be nothing short of miraculous compared to some of what had been going on previously. The result was that both children and staff were noticeably happier and the general tone of the classroom was lighter and easier.

We also put a few common sense health and safety routines in place which had been broadly absent before such as an appointed member of staff checking the classroom for dangerous things laying around at the start and at key points during the day, for example pairs of scissors, and then putting these in the stationary cupboard which was kept locked.

The rest of the school also noticed that the chaos was diminished in this part of the building and posed the question, how is this being achieved? Is it bribery or perhaps hypnotism? No, this was an example of therapeutic practice being done by a small team of people.

It should be evident to most reading that the restraint heavy practice that was previously used in that part of the school was *poor practice*. Both children and adults lost out because of this due to it being quite a stressful and unpleasant working environment for all involved. A shift in attitude and how you work as a team and the attitude that you take to the kids can make an astonishing amount of difference. Have a cool minded think; *what do you bring to the classroom?*

This is only a brief taster of what therapeutic practice means and how it can be implemented. If you reflect on your own practice and that of your colleagues, you can ask yourself how you can be more therapeutic in tone in how you interact with the children. You may choose to make your practice more therapeutic in tone and you may be surprised at the results a few simple changes in attitude and action yields.

None of the above is to encourage that we let poor behaviour pass amongst the children, but it is imperative to consider the motivation for the poor behaviour. Is it because of serious trauma that has happened to the child and the resultant internal chaos that arises? Is shouting at them the best way to deal with this or might a more friendly chat be appropriate?

There are other methodologies such as TCI (Therapeutic Crisis Intervention) which is popular in America that has a structured approach to de-escalating a child before physical intervention is required and a structured approach to discussing what happened to the child directly afterwards.

An in depth discussion of the various systems is perhaps beyond the scope of an introductory chapter to the topic such as this but if you are interested in the various therapeutic approaches, there is a body of literature on the subject and I encourage you to go down that particular rabbit hole of research and knowledge and see what you can apply to your immediate environment to allow it to be more harmonious.

3.8 Who does what? What do these job titles mean?

This section of the book is hopefully self-explanatory from its title! If you are fairly new to education, you may hear a few job titles mentioned and not really know what they mean. If you have a look through this section, there may be a brief explanation that will give you a helpful outline of what that person does.

A lot of the time, if you are curious to know more about what someone with a specific job title does, if you ask them, many people will be happy to explain in a bit of detail what they do. You may even be able to spend an afternoon shadowing them so that you can get a really good idea about how things work. If shadowing a few different people in your workplace is feasible, it really is an excellent way to get to understand how things work and of course, to get to know people.

SENCO

The SENCO is an important person in any school. A school has a statutory requirement (meaning it is the law) that they must have an appointed SENCO. The SENCO (at the time of writing anyway) must be a qualified teacher (QTS or QTLS). The SENCO must have completed or be working towards completing the National Award for SEN Coordination, which is a postgraduate qualification at the same level as a master's degree (Level 7), although this may change. The name SENCO is a contraction of SEN COordinator.

The role of the SENCO can vary wildly between different schools and whilst the description of the job may seem fairly standard, the SENCO role is quite fluid in practice in my personal experience. In some schools, the SENCO can become a sort of drop off person for children that are being disruptive in classes. The SENCO then has to contain those children whilst trying to do their other duties. This is, in my opinion, the least effective way to deploy a SENCO.

In theory, the role of the SENCO should be to serve as a hub for all things SEN within a school. They should be the point of communication for parents, social workers, the local authority etc in order to coordinate efforts and ensure that things are being provided as intelligently for a child as possible.

The SENCO will also usually be responsible for the annual review of the EHCPs of children; they will sometimes be responsible for providing training for staff on how to deal with specific types of SEN or how to meet the needs of specific children; they may start the ball rolling for an assessment on a child to see if they have a particular type of SEN; the list goes on.

The SENCO often has a heavy workload and has to be quite expert in prioritising tasks and switching between them to make sure that things do not go awry.

The SENCO is a good person to get to know in your school. In theory, you should be able to ask them about the child or children that you work with and they should be able to give you a few useful pointers and ideas. This can be a handy thing to be able to do, so it is worth getting to know the SENCO if you have the opportunity.

DSL

If you have read the section of the book on safeguarding you should already have an idea what a DSL is. This stands for Designated Safeguarding Lead.

The DSL is the person in the school who should be your go to with regards to any concerns you might have about a child's welfare or well-being. If you have any nagging worries about any of the children you work with, it is the DSL who you should go and discuss it with.

Like all specialist roles, the longer the person has been doing it for, theoretically the more they should know about it. The DSL should be able to provide fairly rapid advice to you on safeguarding and should certainly be able to make a well informed judgement call on when to escalate something and when to monitor a situation.

The DSL should always advocate that things you raise as safeguarding concerns should be properly recorded and held on record. Some schools have an electronic system solely for this purpose, some have a paper based system. Make sure that you know how concerns are recorded, know the local policy, and adhere to it. Children only get one chance at a safe childhood.

Teacher and teaching assistant

As obvious as it may seem to state, the teacher is generally responsible for the planning and delivery of either a specific subject or a variety of subjects, such as may happen in primary schools. The planning is usually done in a scheme of work which will often follow a set format inside a school, but not always.

The scheme of work gives the teacher a plan or a 'road map' for what will be delivered and in what order. This will usually reflect the process of building skills and knowledge in specific areas. The best schemes of work are those which the teacher develops themself rather than simply downloading one and putting their name to it.

If a teacher does not have any scheme of work or the teachers in a school do not work to those which they have, I would take this as another red flag. Such practice usually leads to chaotic spaces. The teaching staff may blame any myriad of other factors.

In addition to the scheme of work, a teacher will usually maintain some manner of tracking document which details the progress of the individual learners against their scheme of work. Sometimes this will be RAG rated or some similar method, whereby children will be rated as being secure in their knowledge of a specific area of learning, ongoing (or progressing or emerging in their learning) or not yet secure in this area.

You might expect to see a series of checkboxes that at the start of a scheme of work being delivered, may be largely red or not secure and over the course of the year become Green or Secure with some variation due to ability and prior learning of the children in the class. Not every kid will progress at the same speed and this may be especially so in an SEN setting. Some children in SEN may have very different abilities in different subjects rather than a fairly even distribution of skills.

Such a tracking document should be kept with the scheme of work ready for inspection to demonstrate that not only has planning been done, it is being used, and the progress of the learners is being tracked. A progress tracker may also be kept in the front of a learners work folder so that they can visually see how much progress they have made. This will be useful for some learners who like this form of feedback.

You would expect such documents to be checked internally by a senior member of staff on a regular basis to ensure that teachers are doing their jobs properly. These will also be checked by external people such as **ofsted inspectors** and may well be looked at by interested parties from the local authority or sometimes even parents. Transparency in such matters is to be encouraged as an unwillingness to share such documents will usually be taken as a strong sign that the teacher is not doing their job properly or has something to hide.

The teacher will also be responsible for organising and deploying teaching assistants in the classroom. This may take the form of briefing them at the start of the day that *x learner* will require additional support in maths, or *y learner* will require a certain TA to do an intervention with them at 11:00 or that a specific TA will need to check in with a child who is currently experiencing some unhappiness or upset.

If teaching assistants and similar support roles are properly organised and directed by the teacher, you will generally see a classroom that is more harmonious and children making better progress. This is not to say that teachers must micromanage their teaching assistants, which can be counterproductive, but support staff should not be left to awkwardly hover without knowing what is expected of them or to be left to guess as to what they should be doing with the kids in their class. The teacher has a responsibility to organise the support staff and to make sure that they understand what they need to be doing throughout the day, otherwise the input of support staff can become hit or miss through no real fault of their own.

A similar job title that you may find in the classroom is LSA - Learning Support Assistant. These are often present within a classroom to provide support specifically to children who are identified as having SEN.

Imagine if you will, a large mainstream classroom with 30 children and one teacher to meet all of their needs. A child with SEN may require more support that a single teacher can feasibly supply whilst meeting the needs of the other children. In this scenario, there may be funding in a school to deploy a LSA to work with an SEN child or small group of children within that class in order to free the teacher up a bit to support all of the children in the class.

In the often cash strapped modern school, you cannot assume that there will be funding to allow for having a LSA to support the SEN children who may otherwise make little progress or become disruptive through frustration and boredom.

The slow defunding of schools has led to teachers in some schools actually having to send home begging letters to parents to ask them to donate money so that stationary and basic equipment can be purchased for the class. It is difficult to imagine how this is considered to be progress compared to properly funding and investing in the education system.

Interestingly, some of the wealthiest public schools that are run for profit in the UK are given charitable status and so are exempt from paying taxes on the exorbitant fees which the wealthy pay to send their children to them.

Recently one UK media outlet labelled the suggestion that these very wealthy and highly profitable public schools should have to pay their taxes like everyone else as being *'class warfare'*, which is, in my humble opinion, an interesting way to frame the suggestion that *everyone should pay their taxes*. This is only offered as an opinion by the author. If anyone would care to explain the compelling logic of this arrangement to me, feel free. Answers on a postcard.

Another role similar to the TA is the ELSA - Emotional Literacy Support Assistant. This is essentially a TA who has done some additional training in order to better support the children or young adults with their emotional literacy, social skills and behaviour.

Having intelligently deployed ELSAs who are well organised with clearly defined targets and methods for achieving them is really key to their success and the amount of positive impact that they will have in a classroom environment.

Teachers and the various assistant roles in the classroom will often meet for a variety of meetings in order to do things like gather tracking data for individual learners and see how well progress is happening towards individual targets set for the children. Such data gathering exercises may seem laborious and unnecessary, but in actual fact are very useful as it allows for the school to get a general picture of how well things are going, what is succeeding and what could require improvement.

This sort of data, when collected with purpose and used to inform practice and decision making, can be used to demonstrate your good work to **ofsted inspectors** and to the management of your school. Data can also determine if additional training is required for staff in specific areas of their duties, so it can be quite useful.

Occupational therapist

An OT (Occupational Therapist) is a specialist who will have done some extensive training, often up to degree level or beyond in order to have sufficient skills and knowledge to help children develop in certain areas. Not every school will have an OT, but some SEN schools will and they are perhaps more common in working with primary aged children.

At its most basic, an OT will work with children to help them to perform everyday activities. For example, a child may be identified as having poor fine motor function skills (the ability to do fiddly things like handwriting) or may not be developing at the expected speed for their age. The OT would be able to put in place a structured series of exercises and activities which should hopefully be able to help the child to develop in that area.

Some other areas that an OT might help in include but are not restricted to
- Hand eye coordination (Things like being able to catch a ball)
- Living skills (Things like getting dressed, washing, using a knife and fork to eat etc)
- Spatial awareness (Their self in relation to that which is around them)
- Visual discrimination (some may develop slowly in this regard and may have difficulty in for example, telling shapes apart, recognising similarity and difference)

The OT is a valued member of any team and their efforts to help children develop in their specialist arena will benefit the child's ability to access education and engage in play.

Speech and language therapist

The SaLT (Speech and language therapist) is a professional who is sometimes based within a school (especially SEN schools), but sometimes works outside of a school, for example as part of the NHS.

Some children do not develop at the ideal speed in their ability to communicate and their ability to use language. When this is happening for a child, ideally they would be able to access regular sessions with a SaLT.

The SaLT will usually be a highly qualified individual who will be able to do some diagnostic tests with the child and find out where their areas of need are. The SaLT will then take a structured approach to drawing up a plan for how the child can best be helped to develop. This will often involve the other professionals working with the child, such as the teacher and support staff.

Through targeted and focused interventions as directed by the SaLT, it is hoped that a child who is struggling in their arena will be able to make progress towards their targets and will be able to close the gap between themself and their peers.

Due to the severity of their SEN, some children will make more or quicker progress than others. However, with appropriate support from the adults who work with them as directed by the SaLT, most children will be able to make some progress.

Social worker

Whilst there are many different types of social worker, you are probably most likely to come across a children's social worker.

Their primary roles are to

- Provide support and guidance to a family who may be struggling.
- Assess the levels of risk around a child or their situation.
- Signpost appropriate action to keep a child safe and healthy.
- They may be involved in regular checks and monitoring to make sure that all is happening as it

should be in either a family or a care home where one of the children they work with lives.
- To promote child safety and to act swiftly if a child is in danger to prevent them from coming to harm.

Sometimes they may want to check in on what is happening in education for a child.

CAMHS

CAMHS (Child and Adolescent Mental Health Services) is the name for the front line NHS service that helps and provides treatment for young people with behavioural, emotional or mental health difficulties.

If a child at your school is, for example, self harming and suffers from depression, you would hope that a CAMHS referral would have been made so that they can get some specialised help with the difficulties that they are facing.

Early intervention is very important with children's mental health problems, but CAMHS has been somewhat underfunded so they cannot always respond as quickly as they would like to. Treating mental health difficulties further down the line is generally more expensive to do, so restricting funding to those who would provide early intervention is a false economy.

CAMHS is a multi-disciplinary team which means there will usually be a variety of experts working within one CAMHS team who can all add their specialisms in supporting a child. Some of these roles may be

- Social worker
- Therapist
- Psychologist
- Medical doctor
- Nurse

A CAMHS referral can be made by a GP, but can also be made by a SENCO and some other professionals. This would generally be done with parental consent, where there is a level of concern about the well-being and mental health of a child.

There will usually be a wait for an initial appointment where an assessment of the needs of the child will be performed by some trained professionals. The assessment will then be used to determine the urgency and type of support that is most appropriate for the child. For example, depending on the issue, they might receive:

- Medication
- CBT
- Therapy
- Counselling

3.9 Unions and pay scales

Joining a union is an extremely sensible thing to do. Everyone who works in education should join a union. Everyone who has a job should be a member of a union.

A common union to join for people working in education is the NEU (National Education Union), which was formerly known as the NUT (National Union for Teachers). Other people may want to look at joining a union such as Unison or Unite, but it is up to you to decide what is right for you and to set it up.

What are the benefits of joining a union? Well a really key one for everyone is that union members have a hotline to the union's advisory team. If you are ever in a position where you feel that you are not being fairly treated at work, you are being discriminated against (based on your protected characteristics or for any other reason), there is a safety issue or perhaps you think something dodgy or illegal is going on - if you are a member, you can call your union and get first class advice.

You will be able to speak to their team of expert advisors who will give you sound advice, usually on the spot. If they agree that something is happening which shouldn't be happening, the union will advise you and if required will be able to arbitrate between you and your employer.

Never underestimate the value of this service. It is completely conceivable, however much we would like it not to be the case, that some employers are simply not as nice as they could be and don't treat their workers as well as they deserve to be treated. The unions have your back in these circumstances.

Dealing with a less than perfect employer all by yourself can be problematic. You may find yourself up against a team of people who are skilled in championing the interests of the boss (whether they are right or wrong). You may not do too well by yourself under these circumstances. However, on the other hand, if you have a trained union professional who is on your side, you may experience a very different outcome.

Unions also negotiate pay and payscales for sections of the education sector. This means that there are payscales for various different jobs within education. For example, there is a payscale for qualified teachers that you can progress through over the years with an increase in pay each time you go up a point on the payscale.

There are payscales for leadership roles and head teachers and there are extra payments for additional duties such as SEN allowance, an allowance for people with additional responsibilities (for example, a head of year) etc.

The pay scales have done much to minimise gender based pay gaps in the education sector and to help people's pay not to completely stagnate from one year to the next. Education is a profession that takes experience and qualification to do well and as such, *you deserve to be paid properly*.

Sadly, Independent Sector Schools do not tend to follow the union negotiated pay scales, which means that it is very hit and miss what you will get paid for working in an

Independent School. Many specialist SEN schools are in the independent sector. This means that they are privately owned and are usually run for profit, selling their services usually to the local authorities who will place children with them.

Some people will inevitably attempt to tell you that unions are not a good thing and that you should not join a union. Whilst everyone is entitled to an opinion, I strongly disagree with this stance as many of the basic rights we enjoy in the workplace stem directly and unambiguously from union activity.

These rights were often fought for over a long period of time and were for the most part not willingly given to the workforce through benevolence. The unions protect your rights as a worker and will continue to do so for as long as they are funded and continue to exist. Some of the achievements of workers organised by their unions include the minimum wage, sick pay, the 8 hour working day, paid maternity leave, the 2 day weekend, health and safety in the workplace and much more that we may consider part of our basic rights.

In my opinion, not a single person in the UK should have to live in poverty. Not a single person who works for a living should have to visit food banks because the money they are paid is not enough to live off of.

At the time of writing this, current research suggests that there are in excess of 120,000 homeless children in the UK. This contrasted with the fact that the UK is one of the richest economies in the world indicates to me that poverty and homelessness is not an economic necessity.

You may or may not agree with my opinions on unions, and that is your prerogative of course! I personally feel that it is important to highlight to those reading that there are real benefits from joining a union. You may be lucky and never actually need to use their services for advice or arbitration, but if you find yourself in a situation where you do need a union you will be extremely glad that you are a member and that they exist, funded by a small fee from people such as yourself.

3.10 Education, Health and Care Plan (EHCP)

The EHCP was introduced to replace something called a 'statement of special educational needs'. You are unlikely to come across any statements these days but you may occasionally hear someone refer to a statement - most likely they mean an EHCP, in current language.

The EHCP replaced the statement in late 2014. Frustratingly, different local authorities around England do them in different formats, which can lead to some inconsistencies. In my experience, some of the formats for an EHCP are very clear, useful and straightforward but some local authorities produce documents which in my opinion are somewhat murky and therefore less easy to use.

The structure of the EHCP was defined in the 2014 SEND code of practice and it was intended to provide a more useful document with more comprehensive input from a range of professionals working with the child than the previous 'statement of special educational needs'.

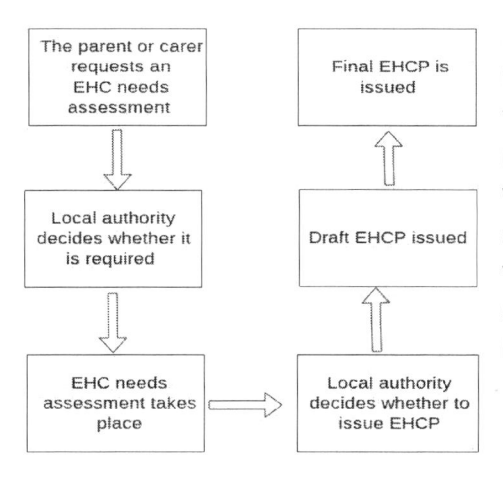

```
The parent or carer           Final EHCP is
requests an EHC              issued
needs assessment
        ↓                         ↑
Local authority              Draft EHCP issued
decides whether it
is required
        ↓                         ↑
EHC needs            ⇒    Local authority
assessment takes          decides whether to
place                     issue EHCP
```

Before an EHCP is issued there are various things that must happen. We will take a quick look at these now before we look at the structure of an EHCP itself.

First of all, someone with the authority to do so must initiate the process for assessment. This may start with a conversation between a parent or carer and the school senco, but if a child is over the age of 16, they may request an assessment for themself.

If the school is not supportive of the request for an EHC assessment, the local authority can be approached directly by parent or child over 16.

Section A

This opening section will contain the views of the child themself as it is regarded as being very important to record the views of the child if they are capable of expressing them. This section also contains the views of the family or legal guardian such as foster parent, primary caregiver, residential care staff etc.

Section A will usually contain a bit about the child's likes and dislikes and their aspirations for the future (which may change from year to year from astronaut to horse rider to computer programmer). Some children may refuse to participate in this and so the information they offer for this may be minimal.

Section B

The child or young person's Special educational needs (SEN).
There will usually be a primary SEN and sometimes a secondary SEN where there is comorbidity (that's when they have more than one condition running alongside each other). The EHCP will often place a child in one of the four primary areas of SEN which we discussed in an earlier chapter - *Social, Emotional and Mental Health (SEMH), Cognition and learning, Communication and Interaction,*

Sensory and/or physical needs.

There will then usually be some detail. This can come from sources such as an assessment made by an educational psychologist. The reports made by educational psychologists are not usually light reading and can use terminology or phrases which people without knowledge of psychology may find challenging. Luckily this should be condensed into a useful summary in section B.

Section C

The health care needs of the child or young person.
This section will generally contain any specific healthcare needs that the people working with them should know about, for example, allergies, epilepsy, and any other health care needs which may impact upon the approach which the people working with the child may take.

Section D

Social care needs relating to their SEN or disabilities

Section E

The outcomes sought.
These will often be larger, more long term goals such as 'for child *x* to be able to participate in group activities with other children by the end of KS3', 'for child *x* to be able to achieve 5 GCSEs at the end of year 11' or similar. These are not always overarching targets and can be smaller ones. The quality of targets put in this section can vary wildly.

The targets which are placed in this section should always be SMART targets. If you are not familiar, this is an acronym for Specific, Measurable, Achievable, Realistic and Time constrained.

For example, *"that Patrick will be able to recite the 10 times table by the end of this academic year". "That Victoria will be able to share a toy with a peer in structured play activities for five minutes by the time of the next annual review". "That Jamie will be able to Highland dance for ten minutes by the end of the academic year".*

Section F

The special provisions required to meet the SEN needs of the child.
This is a very key section and one which is well worth paying attention to.

Section F lists the adaptations or strategies which you **MUST** have in place for the child in order to meet their needs as identified at assessment.

This could be a short and simple list of easy adaptations that must be provided but with children with more complex needs it can be a long and demanding list which can make them only really suitable for very specialist provisions. Meeting the needs in Section F is a legal requirement so ignore it at your peril!! It is highly likely that you will have people in from the local authority to check the quality of the provision and the sort of questions they will ask include *'what are you doing to meet the child's needs as defined in Section F of their EHCP?'.* If your answer is *'I have no idea',* it is possible that things will not go very well for you from there in your relationship with that professional. Whilst it is your whole school's duty to meet the needs defined in Section F, it is not going to hurt if you know about the content too. It's not good to assume other people are always diligent with this.

Section G Any health care provision that the school is required to provide for the child. These might include but are not restricted to: - Medical treatments and the administration of medicines (and staff training that may be required around this) - Physiotherapy/ occupational therapy (OT) - Nursing support required - Continence supplies and routines - Specialist equipment required and or mobility aids - Any other information relating to the healthcare needs of the child
Section H (1 and 2) Any social care provision that must be provided for the child
Section I This section names the preferred learning provider.
Section J This section details any funding that will be required in order for the needs specified in the EHCP to be met.
Section K Advice and information from the EHCP assessment

The local authority will then consider the evidence if there is a case for assessment. If so, assessment will take place by someone like an educational psychologist.

A draft EHCP will be written and if the various parties are in agreement, it will be issued as the final EHCP, which will then be reviewed on a yearly basis to ensure that it is still relevant and needed. Someone can have an EHCP up to the age of 25.

Statutory rights around EHCPs and the process of getting one are detailed in the *SEND Code of Practice*. This can be a very useful document to familiarise yourself with if you are involved in this process at any point as it is fairly 'black and white' in describing entitlements and duties and can potentially be used to remind people of their duties around the process.

If an EHCP is issued by the local authority, the structure should be as follows:

The annual review of the EHCP

There is a statutory requirement for the EHCP to be reviewed once per year. Within a provision with a high number of children with EHCPs this can be challenging to do. It usually falls to the SENCO to manage this process but they will often have to delegate tasks if they are double booked or have a particularly heavy work flow as can happen.

SENCOs have been referred to as 'expert plate spinners', which is not entirely untrue as their workload can be demanding. The upshot of this is that it is far from unheard of for various assistants to be called in to take over in some meetings, so you may find yourself in an annual review meeting at some point making a larger or smaller contribution to the annual review or maybe even leading on one.

The key to being successful in this is **to be prepared**.

Very useful information to walk into an annual review with includes but are not limited to:

- The current educational levels of the child (at the very least in their core subjects if they are doing them).
- Their attendance figures.
- Numbers of incidents (if any) that they have been involved in.
- If the needs of the child have changed since the last annual review.
- If the specifics of section F are still relevant or need amending.
- If additional funding or equipment is required (this may be optimistic or funding may be forthcoming depending on many factors).
- Progress towards the targets in section E; if these are met or even no longer relevant.
- Various other bits of information or figures about the child that you may have access to.

Part of the job of the local authority worker is theoretically to offer some challenge and to probe a little with regards to the child to see if their needs are being met. It depends on who you get, how deeply they will challenge but it is prudent to walk in with a good set of information and a robust understanding of the child in question so that you can answer the questions that may be put to you in a professional and calm manner.

The EHCP should be a working document that staff use to inform their practice with that child. Should the child move on to another provision or setting, the EHCP is one of the key documents that goes with them, hopefully allowing the adults who will be working with them next to hit the ground running and provide the best continuity possible in the way that adults work with the child.

Appendix one - Glossary

This section is designed to act as a quick reference for when you come across an acronym, word or phrase that you are not familiar with. Whilst no glossary is likely to be completely exhaustive, this will serve to demystify some of the language that you may hear in conversations about some of the children that you work with.

ACE	Adverse Childhood Experiences
ADHD	Attention Deficit Hyperactivity disorder
ADD	Attention deficit disorder (seldom used now)
ALS	Additional learning support
APD	Auditory Processing Disorder
AR	Annual Review - the yearly meeting to discuss and update someone's EHCP.
Areas of need	Four categories used to describe someone's SEN. They are: communication and interaction, cognition and learning, SEMH, sensory and/or physical needs.
ASC	Autistic Spectrum Condition
ASD	Autistic Spectrum Disorder (ASC is considered a nicer term).

Asperger's Syndrome	A form of Autism, part of the higher functioning side of the Autistic Spectrum. Less often used now.
Attachment disorder	The resulting set of psychological issues that can arise as a result of proper attachment not happening with a primary care giver in the early years.
Baseline assessment	The initial assessment which is done on a child to determine their levels in academic subjects or other areas of their development.
BSL	British Sign Language - gestural communication used by some people.
BSP	Behaviour Support Plan
CAF	Common Assessment Framework
CAMHS	Child and Adolescent Mental Health Services
CD	Conduct Disorder
Chronological age	The age that someone is in years, months etc rather than their mental age.
CiC	Child in Care
CiN	Child in Need
Cognitive Ability	The thinking and reasoning abilities of someone
Comorbidity	Meaning that someone is diagnosed with more than one area of SEN, i.e. Autistic Spectrum Condition and ADHD.

CRB	Criminal Records Bureau check - the older name for a DBS, which documents if someone has been barred from working with vulnerable children and adults.
CP	Child Protection
DBS	Disclosures and barring service - the government organisation which issues a DBS certificate which shows if someone has been convicted of offences which make them unsuitable for working with vulnerable children or adults.
Developmental Delay	A delay in reaching the typical stages in development that a child reaches e.g., speech, movement etc.
Developmental milestones	These are certain key points where a child is able to demonstrate a specific skill. The milestones are divided into physical growth, cognitive development, emotional and social development, language development, and sensory and motor development.
DfE	Department for Education
DSL	Designated Safeguarding Lead - who you report any concerns about staff or children to.
Dyscalculia	A learning difficulty relating to ability to perform arithmetic and work with numbers.
Dyslexia	Around 10% of the population are thought to be on the Dyslexia Spectrum which means that they may have some difficulty

	with reading, writing and spelling.
Dyspraxia	A condition which causes difficulties with fine motor control and/or gross motor control. In effect it means the person with it may struggle with some physical tasks.
EAL	English as an Additional Language
EBD	Emotional and Behavioural difficulties - a less commonly used phrase, SEMH is used more commonly now.
ESBD	Emotional, Social and Behavioural Difficulties - a less commonly used phrase, SEMH is used more commonly now.
ESP	Early Support Plan
EHCP	Education, Health and Care Plan - detailed document that tells you about someone's needs.
EYFS	Early Years Foundation stage
ELSA	Emotional Literacy Support Assistant
EP	Educational Psychologist
EWO	Educational Welfare Officer
FAS	Foetal Alcohol Syndrome
FE	Further Education - such as college
FGM	Female Genital Mutilation - a barbaric practice which is illegal in the UK and must be reported to the police.

Fine motor skills	The development of nuanced movements such as can be associated with tasks like holding a pencil properly, tying shoe laces and tasks that could be described as 'fiddly'.
Gross Motor Skills	The motor skills associated with whole body movement activities such as swimming, running, jumping etc.
HE	Higher Education, such as university.
HI	Hearing Impaired
HLTA	Higher Level Teaching Assistant
ICP	Individual Care Plan
IEP	Individual Education Plan - A plan developed for a single child to best meet their needs and help them overcome their personal challenges.
IPP	Individual Pupil Profile
Irlens syndrome	A perceptual processing disorder which makes it difficult for a person to process visual information.
Intervention	A structured activity or course of activities that are designed to help a learner with one or more areas in which they struggle, i.e. literacy and numeracy, emotional literacy, anger management, self esteem etc.
JHS	Joint Hypermobility Syndrome
KCSIE	Keeping Children Safe In Education - a key piece of legislation around the risks

		and threats that children can face.
KS	Key Stage - Primary and secondary education has 4 key stages that the national curriculum is divided into.
LA	Local Authority - An organisation that is responsible for the public services and facilities in a geographical area. This includes assessing whether or not a child is eligible for an EHCP.
LAC	Looked After Child - A child that has voluntarily or involuntarily been removed from the care of their family and placed under the care of the state.
LD	Learning Difficulties
LEA	Local Education Authority
LSA	Learning Support Assistant
MAC	More Able Child - a child working a year or more above their chronological age.
Makaton	Makaton is a communication tool that uses symbols, signs and speech to enable people with disabilities to communicate.
MDT	Multi Disciplinary Team - a group of people from different professional backgrounds.
Mental Capacity	Mental Capacity refers to someone's ability to make decisions for themself.
MLD	Moderate Learning Difficulty

MN	Medical Needs
MSI	Multi Sensory Impairment
NC	National curriculum - the programme of study which schools are supposed to follow.
Neurotypical	A word that describes the range within which the majority of the population have brain function.
NQT	Newly Qualified Teacher
NT	Neurotypical
NVLD	Nonverbal Learning Disorder
OCD	Obsessive Compulsive Disorder
ODD	Oppositional Defiant Disorder
OFSTED	Office For Standards in Education
OT	Occupational Therapist or Occupational Therapy
P Levels	These are measures of educational attainment that are often used with children with Learning difficulties.
Payscale	This shows the range of pay brackets which someone in education can achieve, for example, main pay scale (MPS), Leadership scale etc. Independent schools and free schools may not follow these and may make up their own pay scales.

PDA	Pathological Demand Avoidance
PDD	Pervasive Developmental Disorder
PECS	Picture Exchange Communication System. A form of communication used with some children who are non verbal or cannot write or communicate easily.
PEP	Personal Education Plan - used with Looked after children (LAC) in order to help monitor their education provision. A meeting between a representative of the virtual school and school will usually be held termly in order to review progress against goals.
Physical Intervention	When a child or young person's behaviour becomes dangerous to themselves or others or they are excessively disruptive, it may become necessary to Physically intervene. Be aware of your school's policy on this and ensure that you have had the proper training before using a physical intervention.
PLD	Profound Learning Difficulty
Provision map	This is a tool which documents the way that a school is meeting the needs of the child/young person as defined in their EHCP and what interventions and support are in place for that child .
PRU	Pupil referral unit - a type of school that caters for children who can't attend other schools for reasons such as being excluded for poor behaviour or not having

	a place at any other school.
PT	Physiotherapist
Pupil Premium	A means of additional funding that is available for some children who are SEN or disadvantaged.
RAD	Reactive Attachment Disorder
Reasonable Adjustment	Changes which a school would be expected to make to accommodate for a learner with disabilities or SEN.
Receptive Language	The ability to understand and process what is said to the child.
Safeguarding	Please see the chapter on safeguarding.
SaLT	Speech and Language Therapist. Someone who specifically works with learners to help them overcome difficulties with Speech and Language.
Section F	The section of an EHCP which states what a school must provide for that learner.
SEBD	Social, Emotional and Behavioural Difficulties - a less commonly used phrase now. SEMH is more commonly used.
SEN	Special Educational Needs
SENCO	Special Educational Needs Coordinator
SEND	Special Education Needs and Disabilities

SEN Policy	A statutory policy that all schools must have. This should reflect local and national legislation and outline the school's values, vision and aim.
SEN Register	This is a list which schools must maintain of all of the children with documented SEN. Children with EHCPs will automatically be on the SEN register.
Sensory room	A usually dedicated space within the school that uses lights, music, textures etc that is sometimes used as a calming space and other times to help develop certain senses.
SLD	Severe Learning Difficulties
SLCN	Speech, Language and Communication Needs
SM	Selective Mutism
SMART target	A SMART target is one which is Specific, Measurable, Achievable, Relevant and time-bound.
SMSC	Spiritual, Moral, Social and Cultural education. Something which is supposed to be taught alongside or integrated into the curriculum taught in schools.
SPD	Sensory Processing Disorder/ Difficulties
SS	Social Services
Statutory	Something that must be done
SW	Social Worker

SpLD	Specific Learning Difficulties. This term is applied when someone has generally typical learning abilities in most areas but has a specific issue in one or more areas, i.e. Dyslexia, Dyspraxia, Dyscalculia etc.
TCI	Therapeutic Crisis Intervention - a system of structured de-escalation and Physical intervention that is used in the UK but is more popular in America.
Team Teach	A popular behaviour management training course.
Therapeutic Practice	A way of working with a child which considers their broader well-being rather than just their educational progress.
Transition planning	The plan that is created to help a young cope with change in a structured way, e.g. transition between one school and a new school, transition to adult life, transition between year groups.
Trauma	An event or series of events which put a child in physical or psychological peril which can have long lasting effects.
Union	An organisation that you pay a small fee to for advice and support in the workplace.
VI	Visually Impaired
Virtual School	The department of the local authority which monitors the quality of education for Looked After Children (LAC)
VPD	Visual Processing Disorder

YOS	Youth Offending Service
YOT	Youth Offending Team
YP	Young People/ Person

Appendix two - Relaxation techniques

This technique, if learnt and done correctly can help lower your stress levels, it may increase your personal happiness, and can help with insomnia. Each step must be practised properly, until the technique is perfected.

We begin with simple physical relaxation. Sit in a chair, with feet on the ground, the back reasonably straight and the hands resting in the lap, palms facing upwards (or you can lay down flat on your back if you prefer, on a Yoga mat or other comfortable surface). Why palms upwards? It makes it easier to relax the hands and arms this way as there is less tendency to grip onto any surface below, such as the knees or thighs.

Starting with your toes, consciously untense all of the muscles. Then work your way through your feet, your legs and so forth until you reach your spine and neck taking your time to untense all of the muscles so that eventually you feel limp and relaxed. This may take some time to do initially but it becomes easier with practice.

Some people do not learn to relax their muscles and are in a constant state of tension. If you find difficulty in relaxing at will, you can tense one part of your body, for example your left foot and calf as much as possible and then slowly allow the area to untense until it is completely relaxed.

Take your time to relax properly. It helps to begin with if you will not be interrupted (set your phone to silent perhaps), but with sufficient practice interruption and external distractions will not make a major difference.

When you have done the relaxation technique we can begin the fourfold breath. Breathing should be done through the nose and not the mouth if possible. The fourfold breath usually works best with the eyes closed when you are beginning this practice.

1. Exhale until the lungs are completely empty. This should not be strained, but a smooth slow movement of breath. The muscles in your chest and stomach should not be strained or tensed whilst doing this and you should try to relax them whilst performing this.

2. We take our first breath of the fourfold breath. Inhale deeply in an even and slow movement of the lungs. The stomach should be allowed to expand whilst this happens as it gives greater capacity to the lungs. To begin, this should be done on a slow count of four.

3. When the lungs are completely full, we hold the first breath on the same slow count of four that we inhaled on.

4. We then slowly exhale on the same slow count of four, in an even, unforced exhalation until our lungs are completely empty. The stomach should pull inwards a little as the lungs empty as this helps completely empty them.

5. We then hold our exhalation (completely emptied lungs) on the same slow count of four, without straining.

6. We then return to the start and inhale again working through all of the
steps.

This should form a slow even rhythm of completely filling and completely emptying the lungs. It should be performed as slowly as you can whilst still remaining comfortable and unstrained/ tense. At no point should this technique be forced or strained. This can be done for 5 minutes or half an hour or longer as necessary. As you progress with this practice you should be able to train yourself to do it for longer and longer periods of time.

When the onset of stress, worry or tension is suspected, this technique should be performed straight away if you can. This technique should also be performed if you feel yourself having unnecessarily negative thoughts or difficulty sleeping.

Practise it like you would any other new skill. You will have to persevere with it. Whilst not impossible, it is unlikely that you will master this technique the very first time you try, so stick with it and practise regularly.

Next step. When you are reasonably comfortable stilling the body as outlined above with the fourfold breath we must practise stilling the mind. Perform the relaxation technique followed by the fourfold breath.

The mind often chatters to itself. The mind can pursue negative thought trains that result in feelings of stress and physical discomfort without achieving anything constructive for our lives or solving any of our problems. We can even unconsciously train ourselves to do this for much of our waking time and fall into this as a habit. It is possible even to feel out of control of what paths our mind follows. So our next task is to learn to be still in our minds.

Any habit that is learnt can be unlearnt.

The fourfold breath is a good preliminary to this as we can focus on the beats of the fourfold rhythm as we breathe, instead of mundane thoughts such as conversations or arguments we may have had, deadlines at work, housework or any number of other distractions.

We now turn our focus to stilling mundane thoughts that enter our minds of our everyday lives.

If thoughts about work, family, bills or our day to day routines start to enter our heads, we should gently turn our attention back to our practice, and instead allow ourselves to move towards a state of mental stillness. If you have difficulty stopping a particular thought, allow it to run its course and then simply return to your stillness.

We should not struggle to stop a thought, but rather simply allow a sentence to end and then put a full stop after it and release it.

The thoughts that arise are not usually external to us and arise from a restless portion of our mind. Our aim is to train that portion of the mind to allow itself rest and happiness as it deserves.

If we compare our mind to a summer day sky, picture the blue background and the wispy clouds that travel in front of it. Do we look at a cloud and boldly state that this is the sky? Probably not. The cloud passes across the sky and eventually goes on its way.

In the same way, your self is not the sometimes negative thoughts that intrude on the clear sky of being. Simply allow these thoughts to move away so as to not obscure the natural radiance of your mind.

With practice, this becomes easy. It is worth taking the time to master this technique as there are multiple benefits.

After you have physically relaxed and are successfully performing the fourfold breath, allow all thoughts to leave your head. If an inner voice does emerge, try not to internally verbalise the thoughts that may arise in sentences, simply allow the impulse to ebb away without pursuing it or grasping it as something that must be followed.

Some people additionally find it useful to use visualisation techniques along with the fourfold breath to quiet the mind.

Some people visualise a large two dimensional square inside their minds and imagine that they are drifting along each edge of the square with each of the four breaths of the fourfold breath.

Training yourself to visualise on command can for some be initially difficult, but it becomes easier with practice. It is not essential at this stage of your practice but some will find it an invaluable method to help still the mind during these exercises.

If these techniques are sincerely practised daily you may find that you are able to go forth in a state of calm in order to better meet the events of your days. Set aside some time every day without exception. As little as 5 to 15 minutes dedicated to this per day are better than no minutes at all.

The perfect time to do this is when you first rise in the morning. Some will state that their day is so busy they cannot possibly do this. I would suggest that setting your alarm 15 minutes earlier each day is no hardship in exchange for a more calm and peaceful life.

These techniques, as they do not involve physical movement or asanas, can be practised anywhere. On the train if you commute on a train, at many places of work during break time, laying in bed, anywhere where it is safe to do these simple techniques.

Appendix three - Further resources

This list is by no means exhaustive, but if you have a particular interest in an SEN or condition, some of the following sources may be able to provide more information to you. This list is correct at the time of publishing but website addresses etc can change with time, so hit the search engines as required.

I feel it important to point out that the author does not necessarily endorse or agree with all views of any of the organisations listed, so in the highly unlikely event an organisation starts, for example, to spout transphobic views, I am not with those guys and I was unaware at the time of publishing.

Autism

https://www.autism.org.uk/

https://www.childautism.org.uk/

https://autismuk.com/

https://www.ambitiousaboutautism.org.uk/

ADHD

https://adhduk.co.uk/

https://www.adhdfoundation.org.uk/

Dyslexia

https://www.bdadyslexia.org.uk/

https://www.dyslexia.uk.net/

Eating disorders

https://www.beateatingdisorders.org.uk/

https://www.talk-ed.org.uk/

General resources

https://www.nhs.uk/mental-health/

https://www.mind.org.uk/

Mental health and depression

https://www.studentminds.org.uk/

https://www.youngminds.org.uk/

Therapeutic practice

http://www.danielhughes.org/p.a.c.e..html